# OPPORTUNITY KNOCKING

## LESSONS FROM BUSINESS LEADERS

AN AGATE IMPRINT

CHICAGO

Printed in the United States of America.

Library of Congress Cataloging-in-Publication Data

LaRocco, Lori Ann
 Opportunity knocking : lessons from business leaders / by Lori Ann LaRocco ; foreword by Dick Armey.
    pages cm
 Includes index.
 Summary: "Stories of innovation and success from some of the world's top business leaders illustrate strategies for identifying and seizing business opportunities"-- Provided by publisher.
 ISBN-13: 978-1-93284-187-9 (hardcover)
 ISBN-10: 1-932841-87-3 (hardcover)
 1. Success in business--Case studies. 2. Leadership--Case studies. I. Title.
 HF5386.L266 2014
 650.1--dc23
                    2013036473


10 9 8 7 6 5 4 3 2 1

B2 Books is an imprint of Agate Publishing. Agate books are available in bulk at discount prices. For more information visit agatepublishing.com.

*I have learned in my life that some of the greatest pearls of wisdom come out of the mouths of babes.*
*I quote my son, Nicholas, who said when he was 11:*
*"Don't think about the future, make your future!"*
*Nicholas, Declan, and Abby, may your future be full of promise and love.*

# Contents

WITHDRAWN

# Foreword

WHAT MAKES A good leader? We attempt to answer this question on a grand scale every four years, don't we? The candidates and their teams, along with their allies in the media, try to paint us a picture of what we need in a leader; why their guy or gal espouses those things and why the other one doesn't. But that's just politics, and we can't count on what those folks say during the height of the campaign to carry the full weight of truth.

It's not the tangible things, the easy targets, that make a good leader, no matter what the insiders want us to believe. Lori Ann LaRocco says perfectly in this book something that I've been saying for years. It takes an intangible ability and the courage to seize opportunity to make a great leader, not any of the silly things we're made to believe, like who's got the best slogan or haircut. Lori Ann's book turns out to be a brilliant expansion on one of my favorite axioms: "You can't get your finger on the problem if you've got it to the wind."

Someone can possess all the qualities we commonly associate with a leader, but there is one thing that sets true leaders apart from the rest: the ability to seize opportunity even when faced with failure. If this wasn't something required of leaders, then how would wars be won? How would injustices be righted? Every time a soldier leaves the safety of his base or even his foxhole to carry out a mission, there's a chance he will fail. He might take too long to decide whether it's worth it to abandon his safety and miss the opportunity all together. He might decide at the outset that the risk of failure is too great despite the necessity of success. These are unacceptable options. That's why the soldier who moves without hesitation to accomplish the mission is often the most successful. He catches his enemies by surprise with his swiftness and catches his superiors' attention with his courage. There's a leader, even if he's just a private.

Leaders aren't afraid to fail. They recognize there can often be a long-term benefit to failure. A "good loss" is a term that coaches use to help the team to remember that they aren't invincible. The fear of failure is also assuaged by a good leader when he or she is able to recognize that the opportunity cost of complete inaction is often more costly than failure itself. This is because the opportunity cost of inaction includes the chance and rewards of success.

Those in positions of leadership are often far too concerned about how the history books will remember them. What many don't realize is that if this is their number-one concern before they make a decision, they are likely to be remembered poorly, if remembered at all. The people profiled here in Lori Ann's book aren't here solely because they succeeded. Their profiles are here because they had the courage to accept failure as a possibility. Having that intangible character trait is often the difference between success and failure anyway.

So what are we really looking for in a successful leader? I believe that history has taught us that we aren't so much looking for someone with a track record of success, but maybe someone who, win or lose, knows that the first step toward failure is inability to make decisions.

Lori Ann has put together an impressive anthology. I challenge you to read the stories of these leaders and identify choices they made where decisiveness and courage were the difference between their current place in history and a place in the realm of the forgotten.

**Dick Armey**

*Dick Armey is the former House Majority Leader (1995–2003) and was one of the chief authors of the Contract with America. He is the former chairman of FreedomWorks.*

# Preface

I F I WEREN'T a journalist, I would probably be a psychologist, because I am fascinated by how people think. For better or worse, how we think has a direct impact on the future. What I have learned over years of covering both local and business news is that personal decisions drive one's destiny. There will always be surprises that are out of your control. But, just as you will not grow your money if you keep it on the sidelines, you will not build your future if you simply wait for an opportunity to come to you. You need to *create* your opportunity.

As Peter Ensel, a former journalism professor of mine, once told me, a great story can be at the end of your nose—you just have to keep your eyes open. This advice can also be applied to any opportunity. Opportunity is often linked to positive situations. However, it can sometimes be found during moments of utter despair and hardship. You've heard the phrase "a frown is an upside-down smile." Opportunity is there, even in your darkest hour. From Harold Hamm, the oilman who conquered poverty, to Alan Mulally, the leader of Ford's storybook turnaround, the people profiled in this book have seized opportunities in unlikely places. They are candid in sharing their experiences and passionate about the strategies they've employed to create success.

Although not everyone can come up with the "next big thing," there are many doors of opportunity out there waiting to be opened. Have you ever asked yourself, "Why didn't I think of that?" I certainly have.

Sometimes we make things too complicated for ourselves to grow. Each of us has a leader inside, I think we just forget that sometimes.

All too often we choke down the feelings that come from our gut because they lead to ideas that are unconventional. Maybe you're afraid of getting rejected or don't have the support of your family or friends. Maybe you're thinking to yourself, "I'm too busy with my kids or my job to even try." These are mental roadblocks that you need to get around. I had one month to write my first book, *Thriving in the New Economy*. Yes, a month. It was the deadline I was given, but I was up to the task. I could not take off time from my day job, so I wrote my book during my "off" hours. With my trusty digital tape recorder, I interviewed my contacts on my way to and from work. After my three kids went to bed, I wrote. I woke up two hours before my family to write again so this wouldn't disrupt our morning routine (and they wouldn't interrupt me). I had the drive and determination to get it done, and I did.

Success depends on your belief in yourself. The people in this book all share key traits, including passion, persistence, and confidence. Their knowledge of their subjects surpasses that of their competitors, but *how* they execute their ideas is what makes them successful. You could have the next great business idea, book, movie script, or song, but if it's sitting in a desk drawer or still in your head, no one will ever know. The future may be look hazy, even dense with fog, but there is a beacon of light burning within you. It's time to open that door and let the flame burn bright. Opportunity is knocking.

# 1   The Opportunity Pyramid

O VER THE COURSE of my two-plus decades as a television journalist and writer, I've interviewed businesspeople ranging from
the owner of a corner deli to the billionaire CEO. At speaking
engagements around the United States for my books *Thriving in the New
Economy* and *Dynasties of the Sea*, I have had the privilege of meeting
CEOs, small businessmen, and aspiring entrepreneurs, and they all ask
me the same questions: "How do leaders think?" and "What kind of
strategies do they use?" I have found my answers are always the same,
and they have ignited a spark in me that led me to write this book.
Though the amount in their bank accounts may vary hugely, the leaders
I have interviewed all share common strengths that are responsible for
their success.

The ah-ha moment came to me one night while traveling back from
Florida after speaking in front of 500 small businesspeople. I was stuck
at the Miami airport, and as I sat on the floor surrounded by other
stranded travelers, I reviewed the conversations I had earlier in the day. I
realized that the strategies that I had described in my keynotes were not
associated with a particular industry. They stood alone, relying on a set
of fundamentals that were universal. Each of the leaders I had described
built one of these strategies upon the next in order to achieve success.
I broke down the process through which these leaders define and then
take opportunities, and formed what I call the opportunity pyramid.

The opportunity pyramid shows you how to identify and act upon
opportunities at any stage in your career. Each chapter of this book will

show you how to create success within a particular layer, or stage, of the pyramid. Each chapter focuses on one leader who analyzed the competitive landscape and seized a particular opportunity (important things to do regardless of one's level). On this journey, you'll learn strategies from Harold Hamm, America's richest oilman, who has a high school education; Ralph Schlosstein, a private equity titan; Steve Case, the legendary Internet entrepreneur; and Lisa Stone, Elisa Camahort Page, and Jory Des Jardins, the three founders of the Internet powerhouse BlogHer. You'll also learn from auto executive Alan Mulally; finance chief Ron Kruszewski; and another private equity giant, David Rubenstein, who blazed the trail in China long before anyone else ventured into the Middle Kingdom.

While this book focuses on leaders in diverse industries, it is ultimately about what all good leaders share. Although their reasons to embark on their careers were all different—from leaving a stable job to pursue happiness to being dissatisfied with a current career to rebuilding a dynasty that had crumbled after years of straying from its core principles—when you strip away the particular industry and motivations, these people all used the same strategies to build success. Each went through the same critical decision-making process in building each layer of his or her pyramid.

This book is also about the qualities of leadership, which are not measured in monetary success. Leadership has no price tag. It comes from within. You own it. You develop it. How you define who you are and execute your plans define you as a leader. Empower yourself with the confidence that you can achieve what you set out to do. It all starts with creating and developing your own opportunity pyramid. The motivation behind creating your pyramid may be different from the motivations in this book, but the formula you will use is the same.

## LET'S GET BUILDING

In the great pyramids of Egypt, each layer is carefully placed on top of the layer beneath it in order to create a structure that is perfectly oriented to the four points of a compass. In the same way, the opportunity pyramid will help you build a structure upward from a solid basis. It will firmly root you and then point you in the direction of your goals.

There are seven layers in the opportunity pyramid:
- Fortify your foundation—know yourself
- Build your knowledge
- Define your opportunity strategy—and stick with it
- Fuel your passion
- Stay the course
- Execute—pay attention to the details
- Think ahead—world domination

## THE OPPORTUNITY PYRAMID

Think ahead—world domination

Execute

Stay the course

Fuel your passion

Define your opportunity strategy—and stick with it

Build your knowledge

Fortify your foundation—know yourself

### Fortify Your Foundation—Know Yourself

There is no one-size-fits-all strategy for success. To start the process of building your pyramid, you need to know yourself, so you can identify your strengths and weaknesses and can decide if you have the competitive edge when assessing a certain opportunity. How can you distinguish between a good opportunity and a bad one if you don't know what you want to achieve or how you are going to go about it?

## Build Your Knowledge

Building your knowledge is the next level of the pyramid. You need to be more than competent. You have to strive to be the best. This applies to people at every level of business. Your boss wants the best out of you because an organization thrives when its employees execute at a high level. If you are a small-business owner, you not only want yourself to be a top performer, you want your employees to work hard and excel. In order to be successful you have to be at the peak of performance. That's a necessary ingredient in service. This level is also essential to the aspiring entrepreneur, who needs to sharpen his or her skills in order to take the plunge.

## Define Your Opportunity Strategy—and Stick with It

The knowledge-building process leads directly into the next layer, defining your opportunity strategy. What does opportunity mean to you? You may be at a crossroads in going to the next level of your business, career, or aspiring career, so defining a strategy may mean taking radical steps to reset your course. You internalize whatever life lessons and experiences come your way, so garner from them the courage and the conviction to define your opportunity strategy and stick with it.

## Fuel Your Passion

Passion is the fuel that keeps you going and inspires you on your way, but being passionate is not the same as being impulsive. The thrill of knowing you are on your way can become intoxicating. You must be sure that your execution is dead on. You can't let the emotional highs and lows cloud your judgment.

## Stay the Course

When you set a course, there may be naysayers who doubt you. Hear them out if you respect their opinions, but if you don't agree with them, don't be swayed. Remember, this is your life and you are accountable for the decisions you make. If you want to home in on your passion and build a business, you need to be comfortable with the path you take. Who cares what the others think? You will see examples in this book of people who went against those who disagreed with their plans, staying the course to come out on top. Remember that in the end, it's *your* blood, sweat, and tears that are woven into the fabric of your business or idea.

## Execute—Pay Attention to the Details

If you want something bad enough, you have to make sure you execute effectively. If for some reason it becomes clear during the execution process that a plan will not work, you have to make sure your backup plan is clear immediately. As Dagfinn Lunde, transport banking financier extraordinaire and member of the board of managing directors for transportation lender DVB Bank, once said to me: "The backup plan has to be clear immediately because, when you sit on that tipping point, you can't wait. Sometimes you have to give up the first plan and go to your alternative plans. You do not want to fail. You just have to find the right way to execute and work on those alternatives to prepare for such an occasion."

## Think Ahead—World Domination

All this preparation is fortifying you for what BlogHer founders Lisa Stone, Elisa Camahort Page, and Jory Des Jardins call "world domination"—whether that comes in the form of expanding your business, getting a job promotion, or leaving your job and embarking on a new career or business. Your apex is what you want it to be. "World domination" could be considered a hefty description, but your definition of world domination will definitely be different from mine. It's just about being the absolute best you can be.

## BUILDING BLOCKS FOR SUCCESS

All of these levels fit together perfectly and erect a strong structure to guide you in your pilgrimage to success. Throughout the layers of the opportunity pyramid, the cement that binds each pivotal step is honesty. All of the leaders in this book are brutally honest with themselves. If you do not know yourself, including your strengths and weaknesses, how can you define opportunity? How can you distinguish between a good opportunity and a bad one? All too often we let the fear of failing get a grip on us. We don't want to try because we are afraid we will fall short. Don't let that fear immobilize you.

Another key ingredient is the ability to look forward, not backward. I, for one, do not live with regrets. No "coulda, woulda, shoulda" here. You cannot better yourself if you are stuck in a self-loathing rut. You have to live in the present in order to create your future. While taking a risk and leaving your comfort zone can be a little unnerving, the rewards can outweigh the costs. You will never know unless you take that leap. When we are afraid to make such a commitment, we make up excuses: "I have no time," "I would but there's the kids," or the confidence killer, "I don't know how." These excuses are just weighing you down. If you truly want to do something, you will find the time and way. You will learn the necessary pieces of information to start a business, get that promotion, or expand your business.

Although there are opportunities to be taken at every stage of a career, true leaders need to create their own opportunities. Being presented with an opportunity does not automatically result in success. It is how you use that opportunity that makes the difference. This book will take a look at the process of choosing opportunities and differentiating good opportunities from bad ones.

There is an anonymous quote that I believe sums up the lessons one learns while climbing the opportunity pyramid: "All of life is a journey—which paths we take, what we look back on, and what we look forward to is up to us. We determine our destination, what kind of road we will take to get there, and how happy we are when we get there." The opportunity pyramid can be your map on that journey.

## INSPIRATION INJECTION

While on this voyage, I want you to be inspired. As a newshound, I'm constantly pursuing inspiration. To get into the minds of leaders, to learn the how and why, is priceless. My conversations with these individuals left me bubbling over with excitement, each leader becoming my new favorite. I am inspired when I recognize their qualities in myself, and I hope that as you read, you too will be awakened to these traits in yourself.

Since I'm a list maker, I have broken down some of these leaders' steps for success in bullet points throughout the book to make them easier to digest. There was so much information from my discussions that I decided to break down the information even further with a special section I call "A Page from My Notebook," which hits on their rules to live by, mantras, and life lessons. The synergies amongst these businessmen and businesswomen are uncanny.

You may be shaking your head right now, thinking, "Sure, these CEOs are super successful, but how can I relate to them?" Well, at the end of each chapter, I describe how the particular pyramid layer can apply to you. This book is partially a blueprint for how leaders can analyze the competitive landscape and seize a particular opportunity, but you don't have to own your own company to put its lessons to work. It doesn't matter if you are a small business owner, executive, manager, employee, or aspiring entrepreneur—you can apply these lessons.

This is a flexible strategy for success, created with the knowledge that there is no one-size-fits-all way to reach your goals. The opportunity pyramid model will guide you at each stage to look within yourself. Throughout this book, you will learn that honesty, confidence, determination, and passion all help build the opportunity pyramid. Just as each of us defines opportunities differently, we define success personally as well. The opportunity pyramid works because it is based on your talents and how you make the best use of them.

This model also recognizes that achieving your goals does not happen overnight. It takes time, patience, and nurturing. You have to analyze your business and goals brick by brick, layer by layer. The pieces need to fit together precisely, or the pyramid collapses. All the layers within a structure need to be defined and strong; constructing and fortifying your career is no different.

So let's get on our traveling clothes and become opportunity vagabonds. It's an adventure on which you'll discover who you are and what you want to do. In this book, we'll be taking off the blinders and rose-colored glasses. We'll be getting out the picks and shovels. It's time for a reality check. It's time to start building.

## 2     Fortify Your Foundation—
### Know Yourself

## Ralph Schlosstein

W HEN WE HEAR the word "foundation," we often think of the
bottom layer of a building or structure. But a foundation is
more than that. It's the layer from which any structure grows
upward. It takes you where you want to go. One of my contacts who has
been able to harness his foundational experiences and parlay them into
success is Ralph Schlosstein, president and chief executive officer of the
boutique investment banking firm Evercore Partners.

Self-knowledge is built on your experiences. For Schlosstein, those
experiences blend policy and market prowess. He worked in Washington during the Carter administration, first in the Treasury Department
and then as associate director of the White House's domestic policy
staff, a role in which he advised the president on economic development, housing, urban development, and the Chrysler loan guarantee
program. Before that, he worked for three years as an economist for the
Congressional Joint Economic Committee.

Once he left Washington, Schlosstein joined Lehman Brothers.
Then in 1988, he cofounded with Larry Fink what is now the world's
largest publicly traded asset management firm, BlackRock. BlackRock
has more than $3 trillion of assets under management.[1] After serving
as BlackRock's president for almost two decades, he decided to leave

and form the alternative investment management firm HighView Investment Group. Believing in his next venture, Schlosstein committed $50 million of his own money to make it a reality. He raised more than $600 million in capital in the fall of 2008 and had an additional commitment of close to $400 million, including $150 million from Evercore. The firm's strategy was to acquire minority interests in private equity and hedge funds and other alternative asset management forms.

But like any good leader, Schlosstein has learned from both accomplishments and setbacks. In April 2009, Schlosstein decided to pull the plug on the fund before making any investments because he felt that the financial crisis had made his plans less attractive, and he no longer felt the original strategy of HighView was the best use of investors' money or his money and time. He returned all his investors' money, as well as Evercore's. At that point, Schlosstein was tapped to be Evercore's CEO.

Using his political and private business experience, Schlosstein has been able to develop a well-rounded view of possible opportunities. This approach to business is his foundation and is especially beneficial when you consider that after the financial crisis, business and politics have never been more intertwined. But you don't need White House or Capitol Hill experience to successfully maneuver in today's business climate. You just need to be able to adapt—to learn as much as you can about policy changes and their possible unintended consequences on your business.

"There is always a 'new normal' and every business has to adapt in order to continue to be successful," Schlosstein says. "In this new normal, in my industry, financial services is going to be a world where there will be more segmentation and specialization in order to grow and seize on opportunity. The big institutions are going to have to have more capital for the amount of business that they plan to do and I believe that will create a lot of opportunity for high-quality specialty firms."

This is where taking an honest look at his strengths and weaknesses came in. Based on the environment that he was in, Schlosstein asked himself what he had to offer that his competition didn't. And in today's world, he found, it's better to be specialized than to be a jack-of-all-trades. "Your foundation is essential for more specialized companies, whether they're businesses like Evercore, that compete on the basis of their intellectual capital, their ideas, and their relationships; or companies introducing new types of capital markets activities that may be more efficiently done outside of the regulated banking world. It is critical to build on your own strengths, and then adapt to the world as it changes," he says.

In order to do this, Schlosstein explains, you need to have a clear strategy that is responsive to both your environment and the relative strengths of your business. "If you do one without the other, you lose. If you create a business plan that is not relevant to the world as it is today, failure is probable," he says. "Similarly, if you figure out what is going to work today you need to make sure your decisions are competitive for that specific strategy. If you are not competitive you could also lose."

## KEY INGREDIENTS FOR BUILDING A BUSINESS FOUNDATION

A solid foundation contains several key ingredients. One of those ingredients is an ability to focus on the long term. According to Schlosstein, this approach can sometimes make you "look like a chump" if your short-term returns take a hit, but it's critical to keep your eye on the future. "The markets that have better growth prospects and are fairly valued today have the opportunity to produce solid returns over the long term," he advises. "You need to be a long-term believer in the things that enhance productivity. Areas like technology, green technology, and energy are three areas that could enhance America's competitiveness, which could mean strong long-term investing opportunities."

Over the course of building a foundation, all good leaders employ strategies based on their strengths. Since Schlosstein is in private equity, his strategies are all about identifying the best investments to make. But these strategies can actually be applied to any type of business, since all business owners and even workers want to grow and gain market share:

- **Set financial objectives:** "You can't ignore the financial objectives. You have to have your view on your expected return; how much capital, if any, that business will take; and, if you are starting a company, what's the burn rate until it gets to an income-producing business rather than an income-eating business. You need to have a very disciplined financial perspective."
- **Focus on present market conditions:** "You need to carefully assess the market environment in which you are competing. Is there really a need in the marketplace for what you are proposing to do?"

- **Look at your company's skill set:** "You have to clearly look at what skill set or talent pool is needed to succeed in a meaningful way in that opportunity. Sometimes you can find the right opportunity but your business may not have the necessary ingredients to successfully capture that opportunity or your business may have some significant competitive disadvantages to be a winner in that market. That is something you cannot ignore. You need to have discipline about carrying forward on the things where you do have a competitive advantage, while ignoring the opportunities in areas where you don't have a meaningful competitive advantage."

- **Execute:** "Figuring out a business strategy is relatively simple compared to making sure that you execute it well. Execution I think is the bigger challenge. The fundamental building block to good execution is a realistic view of what your company is good at."

You can combine Schlosstein's four strategies to form a base identity from which your business or your career will grow. Then, once that base is established, you need to grow a culture that will nourish it. According to Schlosstein, this is key to success for companies. Culture is the glue that holds almost all businesses together. Maintaining culture can be difficult if you are growing rapidly or if you expand through a merger. However, companies with weak cultures underachieve or fail.

## THE QUALITIES OF A LEADER

What are the qualities of leadership that Schlosstein has displayed throughout the process of building his business foundation? Roger Altman, the founder of Evercore who hired Schlosstein, says the characteristics that make Schlosstein special are his values and ethics as well as his interpersonal skills: "He was held with such high esteem at Blackrock because of the way he treated his people. That is also why he made a seamless transition to Evercore. One thing I know about CEOs because I've been doing it for so many years is that the ones who are most successful are the ones who project these values."

Altman added that Schlosstein's ability to be fair and respect people helped him handle difficult people issues at Blackrock. "He was in charge of merger integration. In a business like ours with highly talented, driven people, having good people skills and coupling them with a strong backbone is absolutely vital."

In business, it's your personality and your ability to connect with people that matter. Book smarts are good, but if you can't interact well with people, you will not achieve your full potential. I am a "people person." In my field, you need to be. I go with my gut and listen to what people are telling me. I find that, too often, people are so consumed with what they are going to say next that they fail to listen to others. Listening is crucial in connecting with someone. Because of Schlosstein's ability to read people, Altman says he is a powerhouse recruiter for Evercore, specializing in the firm's hiring of senior-level management.

## BREAKING DOWN THE BUSINESS

Schlosstein listens to his team and then evaluates information he receives to see if it makes sense to make a particular investment. Mergers and acquisitions are long-term investments. Combining companies and making them one is a lengthy process. You need to see if the cultures of the two companies will mesh and see which redundancies are present so you can streamline the new company. You need a critical eye to step back, make lists of tasks, and then decide on the best way to execute them. Schlosstein keeps his foundation solid by acknowledging the highs and lows of the business cycle and how that can impact his planning. Timing is critical in the foundation-building process. "Our largest business by far is our M&A and strategic advisory business. It's a long-term secular growth business; historically, the M&A market in the last 30 years has had 5- to 8-year up cycles and 2- to 3-[year] down cycles. We believe we are considerably through the down cycle and in the early stages of another growth period," he says.

Not only does Schlosstein break down his opportunities by examining them by business type, he also isolates specific factors on a micro level. Schlosstein explains that when his business analyzes the M&A landscape, he looks for several conditions to develop a strategy for growth: relatively stable capital markets, CEO confidence, and the clarity of the economic recovery (over the intermediate term, Schlosstein expects all of these to become gradually more positive).

## POLITICS AND THE BUSINESS FOUNDATION

Schlosstein hasn't worked in government for more than 30 years, and, while he follows politics closely, he avoids trying to influence or guess policy outcomes. He says, "My view is that governmental policy tends to overcorrect in both directions. In the 30 years that I have been in business, I have never gone to Washington to express my view on a specific piece of legislation, even though I know a number of senators and congressmen. I believe no matter what the political outcome, you have to adapt your business model to whatever policies the government decides."

Schlosstein says he's always felt that great businesses adapt to whatever new regulations are placed on them, taking the governmental world as it is given to them: "You do that by figuring out how to adapt through a combination of your own business strategy, the pricing of your product and figuring out a way to maintain a good return on equity within that context. It's quite honestly very hard to affect the direction of governmental policy, particularly in today's world."

## THE NEED TO EVOLVE

Schlosstein also spoke to me about the importance of his company evolving as the environment has changed: "When looking at M&A activity, it is very clear to me that the share of M&A activity is going to the independent investment banking firms like Evercore and that share will continue to go up in the coming years. In 2000 firms like Evercore represented 4 percent of the mergers; in 2009 and 2010 they represented about 22 percent. In 2012, 2013 they represented 24 percent." Over the intermediate to longer term, he says this trend of market share pick up in M&A actually has him bullish on the possible opportunities for Evercore. In other words, though Schlosstein's foundation is strong, it isn't rigid or inflexible. His self-knowledge allows him to tailor his business efforts to new scenarios.

## FINDING AN IDENTITY

Schlosstein's secret to success is he isn't afraid to be himself—he is bluntly aware of his strengths and weaknesses. And more importantly, he knows how to use them. Schlosstein knows Schlosstein. He takes this honesty into the boardroom and beyond. If you do not have the proper skill set to execute an opportunity you are considering, you may actually do more harm than good to yourself or your organization.

Having a clear sense of yourself and your values is one of the keys to success. Schlosstein laid it out simply. If you know what your company is about, create a business plan that is built around your core values, and have the discipline not to stray from those values. By executing on your strengths, you have a better chance to seize opportunity.

A Page from My Notebook: **Ralph Schlosstein**

### Rules to Live By

- Never compromise your integrity: once it is lost, it is rarely retrievable.
- Always strive for perfection; settle for nothing less than excellence.
- Treat everyone with respect.
- Constantly communicate. People perform best when they understand the strategy and tactics.

### Mantra

A great leader is like a great point guard—they make everyone around them a better performer.

### Life Lessons

- Learn from your mistakes; everyone makes them.
- Focus on execution; the best idea will fail if it is poorly executed.
- Focus relentlessly on culture.

## BUILDING YOUR PYRAMID

Running a business is a lot like running a marathon—you're in it for the long haul. No sprints until you get near the finish line, or you won't place in the race. A good leader not only looks at the here and now, he also builds up the strengths of his company over the long term in order to capture future opportunities.

A good business strategy is the backbone of a company. But adjusting a strategy isn't like getting an adjustment from the chiropractor. When this backbone is adjusted, it can sometimes cripple a company. Companies that grow so large so fast can lose their identity. We have seen mergers that were celebrated, only to be demonized later. You need to look at the big picture and acknowledge the individual role of all the moving parts. While these parts of your foundation are all individual blocks, they all fit together just like all the layers of the opportunity pyramid. The success of the whole relies on each individual piece.

Here are some insights, drawn from Schlosstein's career, on how to build the foundation of your own opportunity pyramid.

### If you are a business owner or manager:

The biggest strategy Schlosstein has used to build his foundation is honesty. By taking a hard look at who he is, what his company excels at, and the competitive landscape, he has been able to leverage his company based on its strengths.

No matter the size or nature of your business, begin by asking yourself a series of questions:

### What are the competitive strengths of your business?

Is your business a leader in its niche, or a rising star? If you were a client, would you do business with your organization more than once? Are you proud of the quality of work that comes out of your business? Does your business have a high level of integrity?

### Have you crunched the numbers?

What are your financial objectives? What are your expected returns? How can you, like Schlosstein, develop a financial perspective that takes into account your balance sheet, cash flow, and, ultimately, income?

### What makes your business unique and competitive?

What makes your business stand apart? Schlosstein stresses the importance of looking at the skill set of your staff and company when choosing opportunities. He also points out that you need to ensure your business plan is relevant to current market conditions.

### How would you characterize the competition?

Like Schlosstein, remember to factor present market conditions into your decision-making process. Is your competition too broadly focused? What kinds of services do you excel at? Where is your competition lacking? Is there an opening you can use to set yourself apart and take market share? Use your competitors' weaknesses as a point for you to possibly seize on and fill a void.

### Which of your strengths can take your company to the next level? What are your weaknesses?

Schlosstein says it's critical to draw on your strengths but to adapt to the world as it changes. You need to be nimble. Remember also to admit your own weaknesses—everyone has room for improvement.

### What qualities are you looking for in an employee?

Are you looking for employees who are trustworthy and reliable; who are positive and willing to go the extra mile; who have both people smarts and book smarts? You need to figure out what works for you and your organization, but generally, a combination of talent, persistence, and empathy are a winning formula for employees.

### Are you creating a culture that encourages empowerment and productivity and rewarding people for good ideas and execution?

Are you creating a positive work environment, or are you pitting employees against one another? Making the employees compete against each other doesn't raise the bar; instead, it kills morale and breeds distrust. This is something I have personally experienced and it is a horrible way to work. You shouldn't have to dread going to the office every day. Being competitive is different from backstabbing and lying to get ahead. What happens is the fabric of "teamwork" you are trying to weave disintegrates, and everyone is out for his or herself. Communication breaks down, and in the end the product suffers. Over the years, I have had numerous CEOs tell me they want to make their employees feel like they "own" the part of the business they are responsible for. This is just the kind of driven, talented staff that Schlosstein has cultivated.

The most successful CEOs are not afraid to provide feedback on performance, whether it's praise or criticism. If you have the right business culture and employees, giving constructive criticism helps fortify the foundation and enables the organization and individual to grow. You want your employees to have confidence in what they do, and you want them to know they will be compensated based on performance. This type of culture will help create and stoke inner passion.

### What is your endgame, and how is your company's culture and mission affected by the endgame?

Do you want to acquire other companies? Do you want your company to be acquired? Do you want to remain private or go public? Do you want to expand? In order to achieve your endgame, you need to ask yourself how the firm's mission and culture will be affected by these goals.

### If you are an employee:

Many of these same foundational principles apply to building career success as an employee. Just like business owners, employees need to evaluate their own strengths and weaknesses. What are you good at? What gives you a competitive edge, and how can that attract employers or earn you a promotion? Home in on your strengths and develop them; isolate your weaknesses and work on them.

Whether you have a great personality, work well with others, or can multitask with ease, it's important that you look at your strengths from two perspectives: your own and your employer's. How does your positive attitude or your ability to work on a team contribute to your organization? Answer these questions honestly and then reflect on what that means and what you need to change. Organizations want employees who are positive, team oriented, dependable, efficient, and creative—go-getters who aren't glory hounds (and we all know an example of the latter). Take the time to understand the culture of your organization. Be a team player. The Golden Rule always applies.

Finally, focus on your long-term goals. If you are new in the industry, see if your company has a mentor program or find someone else who is willing to mentor you. You can learn a lot from someone else's experience, and chances are they'll be flattered that you asked. I have a protégé and I always make it a point to share tidbits to enhance performance. I jokingly call her my "mini-me" and she calls me her "work mom." To watch my protégé grow, internalize my advice, and cultivate it into her own brings me great satisfaction. I believe in paying it forward, and this is one way I can do that in my career.

### If you are an aspiring entrepreneur:

Assessing your strengths and weaknesses is just as essential for entrepreneurs as it is for employees. Successful business owners know what sets them apart from the competition. So develop your business plan before taking the plunge. Make sure you also have the capital you need and that you start your marketing and branding campaign. Stick to your founding principles: who are you; what services and products do you provide; why you are a better choice than a competitor? Just like the business owner, know the present market conditions and how you will be competitive.

If you are leaving an organization to go out on your own, your reputation is everything. Don't ever burn bridges or slack off no matter how miserable you are in your current position; you may regret it down the road. Don't develop what many in my industry have called in various newsrooms a "short-termer's mentality." You want to be remembered positively, and if you leave on the wrong note, that will supersede however many years you were there doing a fantastic job.

---

## FINAL THOUGHTS

Once you have answered the questions in this chapter, you will have a solid foundation for your pyramid. Review your list regularly and analyze each opportunity that comes your way. Be sure you have an action plan. Above all, remember that you are in this for the long term. Don't be distracted by the short-term noise. Focus on your future.

| 3 | Build Your Knowledge |

**Harold Hamm**

$K$NOWLEDGE IS POWER, but this doesn't mean you need an Ivy League education to be successful. Sometimes real-world experience is just as good or even better than formal schooling, and the story of Harold Hamm is a perfect example. Hamm, the CEO of Continental Resources, Inc., is also America's richest oilman, with a net worth of $12.4 billion.[2] But the startling and inspirational part of his story is that Hamm has no college degree: he built his energy empire with only a high school education and real-world, roll-up-your-sleeves experience. A decade after starting his companies, Hamm eventually attended Phillips University in Enid, Oklahoma, not to obtain a bachelor's degree, but to take carefully selected courses to formally gain the skill set he needed to build one of the nation's largest oil-producing companies. The story of how he has risen to success still gives me goose bumps.

Hamm grew up living in a one-bedroom home, and was one of 13 children to parents who were sharecroppers just outside of Lexington, Oklahoma. He learned about basic economics at an early age. "It was up to the children of the family to help out. We also had to be sharp enough to provide for ourselves," he recalls in his soft Midwestern accent. "It was tough growing up. But we didn't know it, because many people at that time were in the same spot we were in—pulling cotton and hoeing corn to make ends meet."

From sunrise to sunset when the cotton crop was ripe, Hamm and his family would work in the fields of West Texas. Hamm would begin school after the first snow or after Christmas, whichever came first. Later on, he worked for Pearson Lumber Company. "I worked there for a couple of years during high school," he says. "Some kids worked at the grocery store, I worked at the lumber yard, had a newspaper route, and did an array of other jobs including yard work, mowing lawns, hauling hay, pipeline work, and anything else that I could arrange time for."

## FINDING A CALLING

In everyone's life there comes a pivotal moment when you find your calling; mine came at the age of 13, when I began writing for my junior high school newspaper and discovered I wanted to be a journalist. For Hamm, it was working for a truck stop in Enid. "It was a very fortuitous time for me," he says. In 1962, the energy industry experienced an oil and gas boom in the Enid area. "I noticed right off the bat the oilmen were different from most people I had known. They were boisterous, but generous people—charismatic. I had never been around people quite like that and it caught my attention and interest," he told me.

In high school, he joined a distributive education program and also got a credit for working. Attracted by his new passion for the oil industry and full of natural curiosity, Hamm wrote a thesis on oil and gas. In his research, he studied famous prospectors like E.W. Marland, who founded Conoco; Frank Phillips of Phillips Petroleum; Bill Skelly; J. Paul Getty; and others: "All those legends in the Oklahoma oil fields really caught my attention and interest. I just thought perhaps if you were a little bit smarter than everybody else like those guys had been—as well as lucky—then maybe you could develop a fabulous company or make a fortune in your own right. This grasped my young imagination so I decided I wanted to associate myself with all that was going on around me."

Hamm knew he could not afford to attend college so he decided to follow his passion and work in the oil patch after high school. "I started from the bottom up, working for a service contractor cleaning tanks and doing all the stuff nobody else wanted to do," he explains. By the time he left a couple of years later to join Champlin Petroleum Company, Hamm had worked his way up the ranks to supervisor of this operation in two locations.

At Champlin Petroleum, he worked at the Enid refinery. The job was good, but he missed working in the oil field and thought the labor union hindered his ability to progress. Fortuitously, an opportunity came along that he could not pass up: "I had a chance to buy one small truck by taking over payments from a guy that was about to lose it, and started my own service business."

## THE COURAGE TO RISK

All leaders take risks, but there's a difference between careless risk and calculated risk. At the time that Hamm was growing his business, it was the winter of 1966, and he had a house and a young family: "I had to borrow money at the bank and because I wasn't yet 21 years old, I had to have somebody co-sign my loan. I quickly paid back my bank loan and was making money." Hamm knew that in order to stand on his own two feet, he needed to pay that loan back quickly. His courage to take on the risk of the loan also gave him the confidence he needed to move forward. It was a calculated risk that was successful.

For two years, Hamm was a one-truck operation. He remembers, "I did things a little bit differently than most people assumed. My entire business plan simply was: if I did a better job at a fair price I would end up with most of the work. That started occurring and so I had to expand my business. With no one else to rely on, there were stretches of five to six months I worked without a day off. At that point everyone was so busy, I took on a partner, Les Phillips, and we incorporated and built Hamm and Phillips Service Company from there. This fledgling company became the largest oil field fluids carrier in Oklahoma and today operates in several states as part of a larger public entity known as Superior Energy [Services]."

But even with the amazing growth his company was experiencing, Hamm wanted more: "I was primarily interested in the exploration side of the business. I still had my eye on the goal that I wanted to find oil and gas in my own right. So I just made it a point to learn everything I could from everybody else around me, whether they were in the well-services business; the drilling business; a geologist, engineer, or production worker. I pressed them for information. I wanted to learn everything I could from whoever was around me. In the oil and gas business, people are generous and they want to help you—many became mentors to me."

Hamm credits how much he was able to learn from those around him to his ability to be open-minded. The knowledge he gained helped him start another business in 1967 at the tender age of 22, a year after he had started his trucking business. Hamm named the new company after his young daughters Shelly and Deanna, calling it Shelly Dean Oil Company. That company was the forerunner for Continental Resources, Inc., now one of the largest US petroleum liquids producers. "At first we didn't have a lot of activity in terms of drilling and exploration," he says. "I soon began picking up some leases and did some speculating on them; I also had the inspiration for a geologic concept across portions of Alfalfa, Woods, and Major counties in Oklahoma. I began buying leases to support this exploration concept, which included some producing wells from Getty Oil Company in Alfalfa, Oklahoma."

He continued: "I drilled my first grassroots well in 1971 on this acreage, and it was a good producer. I then stepped out and drilled a second well, a wildcat [an exploratory well that is drilled in land not known to be an oilfield], more than five miles from any other producer in Woods County, Oklahoma. This well produced at a rate of 75 barrels of oil per hour. This field eventually made six million barrels of oil. Although we owned a small portion of all the acreage in the play, it was a nice start for my company and got us going in the right direction. But even with this success I was simultaneously growing two different companies. It was difficult and took a lot of hours, but I was used to working up to 100 hours a week, so that's what I did."

Hamm is a great example of the amount of work that goes into building this level of the pyramid. Working up to 100 hours a week was a great personal sacrifice, but something Hamm had to do. Success is the fruit of labor. I have other billionaire contacts who work their tails off to this day, and they are in their 60s and 70s. They love it; it's part of who they are. The work ethic is ingrained in them. Look at yourself. How would you describe your work ethic? Would you be willing to work 100 hours a week to grow your business? Do you have the passion and fire to keep you going? You will need those qualities to execute on your knowledge. Without them, success cannot be harvested. The hard labor Hamm used in those cotton fields all those years ago translated into a different crop—his companies—and he was going to do whatever it took to make them flourish.

## REMOVING OBSTACLES

Despite the success of Hamm's companies, in 1974, he encountered a roadblock to expansion. There weren't enough rigs to drill his wells. But he didn't let that stop him. Instead, he created his own drilling company so he would always have drilling equipment on hand. The timing couldn't have been more perfect, because in the mid-1970s oil began escalating in price. Hamm remembers, "I bought my own rig, drilled my own leases and those of my neighbors in the field, and grew the business from there. By the time I sold that company in April 1982, we had 11 nice drilling rigs, which brought a lot of money. Later on, in 1985, during the bust of the mid-1980s, I bought that company back for cents on the dollar, along with a $15-million net operating loss that I could use prior to the Tax [Reform] Act of 1986. I built this company up again to about 25 rigs, and then sold it again in 1997 before the crash in oil prices in 1998 and 1999. My good fortune was all based on timing and knowing when to get in and out of the contract drilling business." Hamm understood how the cycle of his business worked. This, you may remember, is something Schlosstein emphasized as well.

Despite the challenges facing the industry, Hamm saw another opportunity to help grow his business—by furthering his education. "I finally had some money and time to do it in 1975. I took advantage of the opportunity and, for the next three years, learned everything I could about geology. I took other classes as well. That education prepared me for what I needed to do to move forward in my career. My intention was not to get a degree; the classes I took gave me the confidence I needed to be a good geologist and the tools and business skills I needed to grow my company," he says.

Hamm never quit working during those years he was in school. Passion fueled him. "Back then I didn't need a lot of sleep," he says. "I was young and I could do it. I'm lucky; I have developed a knack for finding oil and gas. As I began mapping up horizons and formations on my own, I figured out where to drill and make land deals to support my geologic thoughts. I became what is known as a conceptual geologist and explorationist."

Hamm says he "locked on" to his dream and didn't quit until he achieved it. "Persistence is everything in this business," he told me. But despite what he calls his "laser-like focus," there were lean times. In 1986, the market was flooded by oil. "Black gold" collapsed from $30 a barrel to $10 a barrel and remained there long enough, as Hamm put it, "to drown everyone in the oil and gas business, almost." Hamm says that experience helped him learn when and where to cut back as well as when to move forward again: "It certainly helped me develop the tenacity and all of the habits of being a great entrepreneur. Without these qualities, you couldn't make it in this business. During the 50 years of OPEC dominance from 1950 to 2000, many US oilmen simply lost the will to look for oil in America. Most US companies became natural gas producers to avoid the uncertainty of crude oil pricing. Today, when you look at the independent oil companies that have a lot of oil production, you can only count about 10 of them."

## CRITICAL MOMENT

All good leaders must keep their eyes open for trends that could be threatening, and for Hamm, the glut in the oil market at this time was a warning sign he couldn't ignore. This enormous glut began in 1982 and lasted until 2000. Hamm explained to me how he put his knowledge to work: "That was a critical moment for me. Do I continue to drill natural gas or do I start drilling for oil? I decided to start shifting gears. FERC [Federal Energy Regulatory Commission] had handed down several orders that changed the nation from a reserve-based system to one of deliverability only. That single move created havoc for the price of natural gas. It essentially dumped all the natural gas reserves on the market at once. The result was very cheap natural gas prices for a very long time."

It was at this point that Hamm made the strategic decision to focus exploration efforts on crude oil, because he says he felt the intrinsic value of oil would eventually be better than natural gas in the long term: "Oil is a global commodity. Natural gas was a national commodity at that time. As OPEC's spare production capacity waned, oil prices should be expected to rebound. We then did a geologic study on various basins and decided which basins we wanted to be a part of and where to explore. We went to the northern Rockies region of the US to the out-of-favor Williston Basin, a very oil-rich province." Hamm's geology studies were crucial in this calculated move. There is a tremendous amount of risk in oil exploration. There's no guarantee you will strike oil with every well. But after doing research, Hamm and his company felt it was worth the risk to go ahead.

In 1989, Hamm's company found the Midfork Field near Luster, Montana, in the Charles Formation of the Williston Basin. The risk had paid off—it was good oil production: "I felt the prospects for us were great in the Rockies. However, I also was an explorationist. I wanted to find giant oil fields. So while everyone in my industry was focused on natural gas, we continued on our path of oil and large fields. I embraced technology. With every advance in good new technology comes a new wave of oil and gas. So back then we got into GeoGraphix, an early form of computer mapping. It enabled us to expand our searches from one small area to entire townships. It paid off!"

Building the oil arm of his business had its challenges, but Hamm's determination and knowledge got him through. He said he carefully watched how the price of oil was playing out on the global stage. "At many points in my career, we were flooded with foreign oil," he says. "I have mentioned that in 1986, oil dropped from $30 a barrel to $10. It happened again in 1998 and 1999. At that time oil fell to a low of $8 per barrel. Of course, it was done on purpose by OPEC members to put domestic producers out of business. It certainly took a toll, eliminating 50 percent of US oil and gas companies. So you had to learn how, when, and where to cut back quickly in order to stay in business. And you also had to know when to move forward again."

Keeping tabs on oil prices, Hamm made a calculated risk during this difficult time, moving forward with a new technology he had never used before. The geological mapping technology GeoGraphix is a geo-science and interpretation software that helps scientists and engineers evaluate land. It was through learning about and using GeoGraphix that Hamm's company was able to find a unique meteorite impact feature near Enid, which produced 200 barrels per hour in the discovery well. That feature has now produced over 17 million barrels and will probably go on to produce a total of 25 million.

The new technology has also helped open other areas of opportunity for the company. Hamm says, "We used that new method to find other fields in other areas. Employing computer mapping, looking for high structural underground features in the Red River 'D' Formation, we came across an area that is now called Cedar Hills Field." But the opportunity did come with its own set of challenges to overcome. In one formation in the field, they found they could not drill in the conventional vertical method. Instead, they wondered if they might drill horizontally. They tried it, and it worked. "Cedar Hills now contains 250 million recoverable barrels," Hamm says. "This area covers 180 square miles. We started leasing in 1993 and began drilling in 1995 and we are now producing 17,000 barrels a day for our interest of about 40 percent in the entire field. This one decision [horizontal drilling] opened a whole new door for us. We found horizontal drilling would work well in some of these thin-bedded reservoirs of the Williston Basin that had been overlooked by everyone. The success of Cedar Hills encouraged us to look for more 'passed up' large reservoirs." Having the knowledge to try this new method of drilling gave Hamm and his company the edge to drill in areas others had given up on.

## CHANGING THE WORLD

After Continental's success in Cedar Hills, Hamm told his team he was ready to "find the next big one." He believed it lay in a region first discovered in the early 1950s but which was considered in the industry to contain "immobile oil"—the Bakken region of North Dakota and Montana. Because the area could not be drilled using conventional means, Hamm's company combined their horizontal-drilling technique with hydrologic fracturing (also known as "fracking," a technique in which water is mixed with sand and chemicals and then injected into rock at high pressure). Continental's work in the Bakken play has changed the energy landscape. Its discoveries there have been hailed as the second-largest oil boom in history by US energy consultancy PIRA, and the results of the boom have quickly gained traction in the world ranks of oil production. In 2011, the United States surpassed Russia to become the world's number-two producer of petroleum liquids, just behind Saudi Arabia. In October of 2013, around the 40th anniversary of the Arab oil embargo, the United States became the world's top oil producer, overtaking Saudi Arabia. The increased Bakken output continues to slash the need for US oil imports.[3]

Continental's success in the Bakken has helped usher in a new era in American energy production. China is now the number-one importer of foreign oil, not the United States. And the downward projections of US foreign oil consumption continue, with the Energy Information Administration projecting US net crude oil imports to drop 950,000 barrels a day to 7.48 million barrels a day in 2013. In 2014, net crude imports are expected to dramatically drop another 910,000 barrels a day to 6.57 million barrels a day.[4]

Hamm says the US energy renaissance is just beginning: "America's current energy renaissance also includes natural gas, with 125 years of reserves today compared to 7 years of reserves in 2005. Raymond James, Citigroup, and other research firms have recently predicted these new supplies of oil and natural gas will lead to US energy independence by 2020. With the discovery of the world's largest oil field in more than 40 years, Continental Resources is changing the world." He continues: "The Bakken play is one of the primary fields making North American energy independence a reality, releasing us from the grip of foreign oil and providing the template for tight oil production across the globe."

## GROWING A COMPANY AND MANAGERIAL SKILLS

Over the years, Hamm has taken steps to build his own self-knowledge, not just knowledge of his industry. He says, "I'm a believer that you can always improve yourself. I, for one, can see how I have evolved over the years: I'm not just talking maturity. It's the way I look at situations and the solutions I come up with."

One of the areas in which he notices growth is in expanding his managerial horizons. "Not only have I created and grown multiple companies," he told me, "I have gone through tremendous growth myself as an individual. Obviously, you go through different stages, and you have to continually readdress what you are doing as a leader and get ready for the next stage and set of challenges facing you going forward. I've learned to do that. That's the part of the job that keeps it interesting. Not a lot of people do it, and they stop along the way because their lid can't be lifted anymore. I've always liked change and I thrive on changing and growing the company.... This passion is something I built into the culture of my company. Everyone in my company likes change and likes growth. We are a growth company. It is a challenge, but it's who we are. It's been a heck of a ride. Some employees have been with me for more than 30 years."

Hamm smiled as he told me, "Not in my wildest dreams did I think this could happen. My goals have evolved. That's the key to success. You need to be able to recognize when to expand your dreams. Back when I had my first truck my goal was to pay for my little house. The house was not new. I also wanted to get a new vehicle. That was my first big dream back then and I achieved it and created new ones. Even though I had big dreams, I did not dream we would be where we are today."

## OPPORTUNITIES FOR ENTREPRENEURS

Hamm believes the environment for entrepreneurs today is still strong, despite its challenges: "There is still tremendous opportunity. It has not gone away. That's the beauty of America." But with success also comes failure, and good leaders learn from both the good and bad times. Often it's the extreme hardships that you endure that prepare you for what's next. For example, Hamm had 17 dry wells in a row at one point. He says, "I never gave up. Sometimes things don't go your way but they can be the life shapers that prepare you to take on the next challenge.... Hardship sometimes is just as necessary as accomplishments. If it is too easy, you don't learn the skills you need in order not to give up and achieve success."

A Page from My Notebook: **Harold Hamm**

### Rules to Live By

- I have pressed hard to cram as much leadership training into my curriculum as quickly as possible to get ahead of my competition and grow as an effective leader. I have enjoyed teaching leadership through seminars, while honing my own skills. Although I still have a long way to go, I have developed a leadership style that empowers my key people to implement corporate strategies and execute them well.

- A strong capitalistic system for business is critical so that entrepreneurs like myself can and will build wonderful businesses across America. I believe strongly in entrepreneurship, having built a very large company from scratch.

## Mantra

Planning—planning—execution. Planning is integral to good execution. People who come in with their hair on fire irk me. Poor planning on their part does not necessarily constitute an emergency on my part.

## Life Lessons

- You have to base your life around principles: fairness, integrity, charity, honesty, caring for others, etc. If you deviate from these, you are just fooling yourself and setting yourself up for a big fall. I try to practice humility on a daily basis and employ all of the principles I have learned.
- I have learned never to become over-leveraged with debt. I have a signed pledge on my wall that I live by personally. It reads "Neither a Borrower Nor a Lender Be." It has served me well.
- At Continental we have only borrowed meaningfully to develop projects that have already proven to be very economical, with high rates of return.

## BUILDING YOUR PYRAMID

Hamm's persistence has helped him build the knowledge he needed to achieve his goals. He recognized that he didn't know everything and learned all he could from others about the industry he wanted to break into. It takes a big person to recognize he or she needs help. How many people do you know who have tried to go it alone and ended up with mediocre success or nothing at all? A good leader is always evolving, always learning.

One of my favorite takeaways from Hamm's story is his description of how his goals evolved, from seeking natural gas to drilling for oil. I know so many people who have one dream: to make it big, period. That's it. There's no strategy there, no room for growth. They want it now, without putting in the hard work required. Remember that's not how it works. Hamm's dreams started out modest—he wanted his company to do well so he could pay for his "little house"—but by building his goals incrementally, he turned his passion for lifelong learning into a multibillion-dollar organization.

Here's how to use Hamm's story to help build the next level of your own pyramid.

### If you are a business owner or manager:

Hamm would be the first to tell you that real-world experience is key to success. The reason experience is so valuable as a means of building knowledge is that it teaches you to troubleshoot and find your own answers, not just understand issues in theory. Of course, book smarts are essential, but you need to get your hands dirty. Hamm says having that real-world knowledge can help you as a leader because you have experienced what your employees are going through. If a decision doesn't lead to the result you planned, learn from the outcome so you can tackle the problem differently the next time.

Hamm's experiences helped him learn when to move forward again and when and where to cut back. Hamm calls these experiences "life shapers." We have all had them. One of the biggest lessons of Hamm's career is that you should never be afraid to fail.

Another way Hamm supports this level of the pyramid is through planning. This is something anyone can do. Breaking down the steps and calculating risks are two ways in which Hamm planned. He would look at his plans and then evaluate the next step to make sure it would follow logically. This involves a specific type of multitasking: having the ability, like Hamm, to recognize the present while preparing for the future. How do you rate your own multitasking? Do you make lists to keep you focused? It doesn't matter if you are running a billion-dollar-plus company or a small business. You need to be able to focus on the here and now while plotting a course to the future.

As a small business owner or manager, your goal is to expand your company. You may not want to be as large as General Electric, but chances are you want to grow and be successful. Hamm says his knowledge base helped fortify his ability to thrive on change. Hamm is proud to say he has had some employees working for him for more than 30 years, which speaks to a culture that is nimble, responding positively to change. Ask yourself: Based on how long your company has been established or how long you have been at your company, what's the longest tenure of your employees? Is that a reflection of your leadership?

## If you are an employee:

Since you're reading this book, my guess is that you want to move up in your organization. By taking courses to expand his knowledge, Hamm was able to move up the ladder to success. Would taking a class help you in your career? What about learning from coworkers or setting up a relationship with a mentor, as described in Chapter 1? Be a sponge, willing to soak up the knowledge of those who have the experience. Hamm says he worked long, long hours to get to where he is today. And let's be honest, is there really any such thing as a nine-to-five job anymore? You need to be willing to put in the extra hours to get the job done. It doesn't mean you can't have a life outside of work, but you have to show your boss that you're serious. As Hamm says, a strong work ethic becomes part of the journey.

## If you are an aspiring entrepreneur:

When Hamm started, he was just like you: a budding entrepreneur. But before he jumped in, he learned as much as he could about the industry he wanted to pursue. To follow in his footsteps, build your knowledge by making contacts and networking. Listen to people in the community in which you will be doing business. What do they want? What can you do to set yourself apart from the competition? What kind of experience do you have in this industry? What's the learning curve, and can you afford to take that kind of risk? If you make mistakes, learn from them. Understand how you arrived at the conclusion and try not to make the same missteps again. Building your base of knowledge does not have to be a scary proposition. It's amazing how learning something can give you a new perspective, whether it's taking a course to expand your knowledge, or learning from a mistake. This is how people like Hamm have grown and become even better leaders.

## FINAL THOUGHTS

Don't sell yourself short thinking Hamm would have been rich simply because he is in the oil industry, or telling yourself he was just lucky. Neither is true. He is at the top of his game because he strategically built his knowledge and leads his company well. He was not guaranteed success, nor did he achieve it without a lot of hard work. He knew what he knew, and made sure he learned the rest.

# 4    Define Your Opportunity Strategy—and Stick with It

## Alan Mulally

NOW THAT YOU'VE laid the foundation and first layers of your opportunity pyramid, you are ready to start building up by defining opportunity. Each of us defines opportunity in a different way. What is critical, however, is that once that definition is set you should never stray from it. The story of Alan Mulally's tenure as CEO of Ford is a perfect example. When the auto industry faced its worst downturn since the Great Depression, Mulally successfully led Ford around the problems its competitors faced. He was able to do this by renewing the company's opportunity strategy and transforming the organization in the process.

Before that story, though, some background. Ford, like any auto manufacturer, has the daunting task of not only building cars that people want now, but also predicting the future. What kind of cars will consumers want 10 years from now? It's a challenge that necessitates staying connected to the customer, but the American auto industry lost its connection to customers years ago, when it started building cars they didn't want (anyone remember the Aztek or the Pinto?). The industry's refusal to acknowledge its customers' wants and needs showed in declining auto sales. At the same time, Asian automakers were gaining market share, and for good reason: they were manufacturing the cars people actually wanted.

At that time, the story was all about the auto battle between GM and Toyota. Ford wasn't even in the picture—it was a struggling spectator. In April of 2008, Toyota replaced General Motors as the world's largest automaker.[5] But a year before Toyota took the crown away from GM, Ford brought on Alan Mulally as president and CEO of the company to help turn it around.

## FORD'S NEW CEO

Before coming to Ford Mulally worked his way up the corporate ladder at Boeing for 37 years. He started as an engineer and eventually was promoted to commercial airplanes president and chief executive. Mulally was the man many credited as the chief architect for Boeing's soaring success and restoration as the world's dominant commercial aircraft builder. He led the development of the 777, the world's largest twinjet and one of Boeing's best-selling models today.

Mulally told me that he stuck with Boeing for so long because, he says, "At the heart of me, there was this desire to serve or contribute in the biggest way I can." It was his experience as a design engineer that opened his eyes to the essence of commercial airplanes and the purpose they serve: "Commercial airplanes are more than just airplanes; they are about efficient transportation that gets people around the world." You feel Mulally's enthusiasm for the subject when he speaks. He truly believes in what he and his company (be it Boeing back then, or Ford today) have achieved.

"Think about parallels," he explains, "these companies are both about the creation of efficient and safe transportation." Mulally took his strength and experience as well as his yearning to build the most efficient transportation from Boeing and applied it to Ford.

Mulally had defined opportunity at Boeing and succeeded by not straying from his plans. His vision for Boeing was to make it a broad-based aerospace company that could deliver better value for customers on a timeline of "forever." He helped achieved this growth by focusing on the airplanes themselves. His success with the 777 and his focus were two of the reasons why Ford brought him on. They were looking for a CEO with laser focus and understanding, one who wasn't afraid of cutting away dead wood to make way for efficiency. Ford needed someone with the vision to take Ford to the next level, someone who could help them define opportunities for the organization. Ford's product line was bloated and lacked focus. After years of acquisitions, its identity was a hodgepodge of vehicles ranging from Aston Martin to Land Rover to Volvo (though Ford was still faring better than its American competitors). Its essence was lost. It was Mulally's job to bring the vision that would help Ford find its way.

Before I sat down with Mulally, his office emailed me the image shown on page 50—an ad from 1925, to which I immediately gravitated. The ad's message is simple, yet powerful: "Opening the Highways to All Mankind." Talk about a compelling vision. All good organizations have one—it is the beacon that guides a growing company. Some CEOs would have turned down the overwhelming challenge of restoring and revamping that vision, but for Mulally, coming from Boeing, it was a chance to contribute to another American icon.

## GETTING BACK TO BASICS

When Mulally took over, Ford was a $16-billion company but may as well have been a dozen small businesses. The company had no uniformity and was not "best in class" for quality, fuel efficiency, or safety. There was no real synergy. Ford was losing money and market share. It was sinking—fast. Mulally seized the opportunity he saw in this dire situation, even though it meant taking bold steps.

How did Mulally define opportunity in this situation? He decided to narrow the company's focus to the original Ford brand alone. This was a huge decision, and not one he took lightly, as it meant gutting the company of many of its iconic brands.

Mulally and his team went back to basics, defining a vision and then sticking with it. First, they needed to define opportunity by deciding what Ford was. What kind of brands would it offer? They decided to offer a full family of vehicles: small, medium and large cars, utilities and trucks. Second, Ford focused on being best in class for all of its vehicles. Third, Ford ensured its vehicles would be accepted—and adapted—by consumers around the globe. If a model was developed for the US market, it needed to be adaptable to car buyers in other countries.

## OPENING THE HIGHWAYS TO ALL MANKIND

Back of all the activities of the Ford Motor Company is this Universal idea — a whole-hearted belief that riding on the people's highway should be within easy reach of all the people.

An organization, to render any service so widely useful, must be large in scope as well as great in purpose. To conquer the high cost of motoring and to stabilize the factors of production — this is a great purpose. Naturally it requires a large program to carry it out.

It is this thought that has been the stimulus and inspiration to the Ford organization's growth, that has been the incentive in developing inexhaustible resources, boundless facilities and an industrial organization which is the greatest the world has ever known.

In accomplishing its aims the Ford institution has never been daunted by the size or difficulty of any task. It has spared no toil in finding the way of doing each task best. It has dared to try out the untried with conspicuous success.

Such effort has been amply rewarded. For through this organization, the motor car which is contributing in so large a measure toward making life easier, pleasanter and more worth while has been made available to millions.

The Ford Motor Company views its situation today less with pride in great achievement than with the sincere and sober realization of new and larger opportunities for service to mankind.

*Ford Motor Company*

*Owning and operating coal and iron mines, timber lands, sawmills, coke ovens, foundries, power plants, blast furnaces, manufacturing industries, lake transportation, garnet mines, glass plants, wood distillation plants and silica beds.*

FORD ADVERTISEMENT, 1925

Source: Ford Motor Company

Using this three-pronged approach has enabled Mulally to leverage all of the company's assets to serve the different needs of Ford's global consumers: "We realized that although our cars may be the same overall, it's the subtle nuances of taste of our consumers throughout the world that would enhance them. Eighty-five percent of our vehicles are the same but they are customized to the unique tastes and requirements of every country and every culture around the world."

When Mulally was initially trying to figure things out and prioritize what needed to happen, he recalls asking a question of his team: "Guys, how are we doing?" Looking back, this was a pivotal moment. At that time, Ford was losing $17 billion a year and Mulally knew the answers were not going to be easy.[6] But he had the courage to shine the spotlight on the ugly reality instead of letting it fester in the shadows. By asking this question, Mulally forced his team to acknowledge they had to make some serious—and extremely painful—decisions if the company was to survive. He said to me, "We needed a plan to build a cathedral."

Making tough decisions like these is where having a clearly defined vision and sticking to it becomes crucial. For many, the changes at Ford were devastating. But from shutting down facilities and laying off workers to eliminating brands, the actions Mulally and his team took would help boost profitability and create a stronger company over the long term.

When we spoke about these difficult decisions, Mulally told me, "No matter what industry, we want our leaders to be looking through clear glasses and have a clear plan. The situation is not good or bad. The situation is just the way it is. We get to decide what to do about it. We ask ourselves, what is the real situation and what will we do to really prosper? It's all about people."

From the boardroom to the showroom, Mulally emphasizes the symbiotic relationship Ford executives need to have with employees in order to succeed. If workers don't share the same vision and enthusiasm they are let go or they leave on their own. When developing cars the company looks at the wants and needs of its global consumers. In many ways, human capital is even more valuable than monetary capital. The dynamics of an organization are key. Mulally has the personality, passion, and drive—he looks for people like himself because he knows that the success of his company depends on it.

## THE ESSENCE OF LEADING

What makes Mulally special compared to a lot of other CEOs is his passion for making a commitment and sticking with it. A friend of mine who is a manager at Ford told me Mulally's enthusiasm and passion are infectious, saying, "There is no one out there like him." His awe-inspiring drive was the secret ingredient to Ford's turnaround. My friend added: "It motivates you to grab that brass ring. Anything is possible to achieve if you work hard." Another person I know who has spent a career at Ford told me, "I shudder thinking about the day Alan retires or leaves Ford. He is Ford."

So what is the engine behind Mulally's drive? Here's what he told me: "The essence of me is to contribute to a compelling vision. It's about meaningful accomplishments. I have always asked myself, 'What will I commit my life to?' It's that question that has been my steadfast foundation in how I have sought out and seized on opportunity." As he said these words, you could hear the smile in his voice.

This actionable approach to leading is something that even fellow CEOs admire. Mike Jackson is chairman and CEO of AutoNation, the country's largest Ford, General Motors, Chrysler, and Toyota dealer. Jackson has worked with Mulally since he stepped in as Ford's CEO. Over the years, Jackson has seen Ford's dramatic transformation firsthand and told me, "The auto industry and Michigan should build a statue to Alan Mulally, who singlehandedly has led the resurgence of the American Auto Industry. I would be the first in line to contribute to that statue." This is not pandering. Jackson's comment comes from behind-the-scenes experience. Jackson was on the ground floor during the bailout of General Motors and restructuring of Ford. He traveled to Washington to meet with the Auto Czar a half dozen times. Jackson and Mulally spoke on the phone often during this uncertain time.

Alan Mulally showed his leadership and dedication to the American auto industry in his willingness to go to Washington, DC, even though Ford did not accept bailout assistance. He did so because he recognized that in order for the American auto industry to be healthy, all participants in the marketplace need to be healthy. When you are a true leader, the weight you carry on your shoulders sometimes goes beyond the organization you are building. The trail you blaze creates opportunities for others. You break down barriers for all. In the end, when Mulally turned around Ford, his vision for "opening the highways to all mankind" extended beyond Ford's own customers to include his competitors.

## UNLOCKING OPPORTUNITY

When Mulally found out I was writing a book about opportunity, he wanted to participate because of his passion for unlocking and tapping into circumstances. His approach to weighing opportunity is very pragmatic. Mulally looks at the concerns or worries facing the company and turns them into positives. He explained it to me this way: "I like the word 'opportunity.' I looked up the definition in the dictionary, and one of the definitions is 'a good chance for advancement or progress.' Think about how cool that is! The word 'opportunity' is just fantastic. You don't wait for an opportunity. It doesn't come to you when you are just sitting in a room."

Mulally uses the following three-part checklist to unlock opportunities:

- Weigh the risks of the opportunity.
- Be sure all opportunities support the vision.
- Be open to opportunistic gems.


- **Weigh the risks of the opportunity:** Every Thursday, Mulally meets with his team to discuss growth plans for Ford. They look at the business environment: politics, economy, energy, environment, customers, competition, technology trends, and labor. They look for changes, risks, and opportunities in those areas.

   Mulally has a process in place that enables everyone at Ford to identify opportunities: "It's almost like an all-time continuous improvement process on finding more and more opportunity. Then we check that our strategy is appropriate with the business environment, and we have a plan which is a normal business plan of revenues and costs, cash and earnings."

- **Be sure all opportunities support the vision:** According to Mulally, the concept of "opening the highways to all mankind" is Ford's true north. "That's how we measure every opportunity," he says. "That's what keeps us so focused on making the best cars and trucks in the world. That's why we divested all those brands—Aston Martin, Jaguar, Volvo, Land Rover—and focused entirely on the Ford Motor Company."

· **Be open to opportunistic gems:** For Ford and other automakers, this gem should be an emerald—I'm talking about green technology. Innovation is the key to unlocking such gems.

One of these opportunistic gems is fuel mileage. Mulally explained it to me this way: "If you are trying to improve the mileage of an F-150 or a Fiesta, you have to come up with a compelling road map of technology development." From skilled employees to technology, everyone and everything is part of a company's economic engine. Mulally continues, "There are a lot of exciting innovations out there that can help make a car green: you have our EcoBoost engine, lightweight auto-building materials, integrated electronics, and navigation equipment. Based on all these wonderful technological advances you have the transformation of a hybrid vehicle, then all-electric vehicles, and the use of natural gas and also hydrogen. Technologies which are pretty neat are the ones that have multiple periods of goals where you are improving both efficiency and safety." A great example of efficiency and safety is Ford's integrated electronics—how the different technologies talk to each other. He returned to the motto of opening highways to everyone, emphasizing that this is considered in any new advancement: "We heed that statement with every decision we make."

## FOUR BRAND PILLARS

Ford uses the following four "brand pillars" when the company measures any new technological advancement. These four measures can be applied to any organization's pursuit of a better product:

- Quality
- Green
- Safe and smart
- Value

These four pillars are essential to what Mulally characterizes as the unique process of "natural selection" Ford follows when deciding whether to pursue an opportunity, especially a technological one. Consistency is key when following the four pillars. For example, if the company is considering an affordable technology, the savings should be passed on to the consumer. Fuel cells and rechargeable batteries are expensive, and Mulally recognizes this: "You can't make this kind of grand promise to millions of people unless you can democratize all the technology and make it available to all of us. Because if it is only available to a few of us, then we are not really contributing to Henry's original compelling vision, right? We need to open the highways up to all of us." A product that is unaffordable for the majority of people would not be in line with this vision.

In order to apply the four pillars, Mulally's team searches the globe. They look to see what entrepreneurs are doing and where venture capitalists are investing. Mulally's voice was filled with enthusiasm as he explained the process—it's a treasure hunt for him and his team. And like any good leader, Mulally does not put blinders on when it comes to the competition. Innovation fosters competition. When I asked him about innovations from his competitors, Mulally told me that he recognizes that competition is healthy because it pushes the industry toward exactly the democratization of technology he's pursuing. For example, Mulally and his team follow the progress of Bill Gates's petroleum-driven internal combustion engine. "You never want an improvement to pass you by, because you need that improvement every month, every year, in order to continue on your path to continuously improve and deliver that compelling vision," he says.

## USING THE PAST AS A BRIDGE TO THE FUTURE

Mulally was quick to point out to me that all the technology the auto industry is using today was pioneered by Henry Ford. Mr. Ford made electric cars and seats out of soybeans and even ran his vehicles on natural gas. Mulally's respect for the founder of the company can be felt whenever he talks about Ford, the man. Not only has Ford's former vision paved the way for its new one, but the technology of the past has paved the way to the future.

## ONE FORD

ONE TEAM • ONE PLAN • ONE GOAL

### ONE TEAM

People working together as a lean, global enterprise for automotive leadership, as measured by:

*Customer, Employee, Dealer, Investor, Supplier, Union/Council, and Community Satisfaction*

### ONE PLAN

- Aggressively restructure to operate profitably at the current demand and changing model mix
- Accelerate development of new products our customers want and value
- Finance our plan and improve our balance sheet
- Work together effectively as one team

### ONE GOAL

An exciting viable Ford delivering profitable growth for all

### Expected Behaviors

#### Foster Functional and Technical Excellence

- Know and have a passion for our business and our customers
- Demonstrate and build functional and technical excellence
- Ensure process discipline
- Have a continuous improvement philosophy and practice

#### Own Working Together

- Believe in skilled and motivated people working together
- Include everyone; respect, listen to, help and appreciate others
- Build strong relationships; be a team player; develop ourselves and others
- Communicate clearly, concisely and candidly

#### Role Model Ford Values

- Show initiative, courage, integrity and good corporate citizenship
- Improve quality, safety and sustainability
- Have a can do, find a way attitude and emotional resilience
- Enjoy the journey and each other; have fun - never at others' expense

#### Deliver Results

- Deal positively with our business realities; develop compelling and comprehensive plans, while keeping an enterprise view
- Set high expectations and inspire others
- Make sound decisions using facts and data
- Hold ourselves and others responsible and accountable for delivering results and satisfying our customers

**www.one.ford.com**

THE 'ONE FORD' PLAN

Source: Ford Motor Company

However, he also made it clear to me that the organization's lasting success is due to the consumers who purchase Ford vehicles. The relationship between company and customer is critical not only for success and longevity, but also for the company to stay adaptable and innovative. In the end it's the consumers who dictate what they need, want, and purchase. It's imperative for companies like Ford to listen to what consumers want so they can build a product that meets demand.

## STRUCTURE AND CULTURE

In order to take advantage of opportunity and meet demand, an organization's structure is key. Ford may be a global company, but the model Mulally uses to structure his company is something any entrepreneur or business leader can apply. He calls it the "One Ford" plan (see page 56).

The tiered, focused One Ford plan illustrates the culture of Ford. By meeting every week, Mulally and his team get to know each other extremely well: "You know you can't fool anybody. Without leadership sharing the same vision and communicating about how they would execute, the One Ford plan would cease to exist." As with any plan, it must be executed properly to be effective, and Mulally executes it through his example. He is known for his unbelievable memory, able to recall someone after meeting them just once. A Ford employee told me about being "blown away" by his memory when walking with him on the floor of the Detroit Auto Show. Mulally went out of his way to go say hello to a dealer he'd met the year before, remembering his name and the dealership he ran. "It's things like that that motivate you," the employee told me. "He truly cares about the employees. Everyone is important to the overall plan."

Mulally's personality also comes through in his clothing. Sure, all CEOs wear suits, but Mulally has a staple "uniform" for Ford meetings and events: a blue blazer with a Ford lapel pin, red tie, and white shirt. One Ford worker told me it's comforting to see Mulally on the floor of an auto show "getting right in there" and meeting with workers.

By acknowledging the "people" aspect of Ford, Mulally has been able to include everyone at every level of Ford in its growth equation. Looking at the company's brand now, you know exactly what Ford offers and what it is about. The company has opened the highways to everyone by seizing the opportunity to redefine its strategy and not looking back.

A Page from My Notebook: **Alan Mulally**

### Rules to Live By

- Working together works. Include everyone.
- Practice continuous improvement and lifelong learning forever, not just during crunch time.
- Commit to a compelling vision. Develop a comprehensive plan. And relentlessly implement.
- Be open to "gems."

### Mantra

To serve is to live. Be sure you serve your customers.

### Life Lessons

- Expect the unexpected and expect to deal with it.
- Accept a situation for what it is, neither good nor bad, and decide what to do about it.
- Have fun. Enjoy the journey and each other!

## BUILDING YOUR PYRAMID

The turnaround at Ford illustrates how important communication is to creating a solid business and being able to define opportunity. By recognizing its shortcomings and opening the lines of dialogue, Ford has been able to use a laser-like approach to cutting out the fat and building innovative products. Mulally's story also shows that good leaders should have the courage to not only see what business opportunities lie ahead, but also to value human capital and recognize the opportunity a healthy culture creates.

Here's how to capitalize on your opportunities as Mulally has.

## If you are a business owner or manager:

Ford's story is a good example for business owners and managers because it is actually two stories: First, the story of a company that strayed from its mission statement and then failed (Ford before Mulally); and second, the story of how a beleaguered, bloated company was resurrected by redefining the organization.

All the decisions Mulally made were based on the mission statement. There is a saying many businesspeople I know use—"use a scalpel, not an ax"—that describes how leaders like Mulally plan drastic moves. Using a scalpel means paying attention to detail and thinking long and hard before making cuts. Every decision goes back to that central vision. By trimming away the excess that didn't fit with the mission statement, Mulally was able to fortify the company's future.

When you are defining or redefining your company, you need to do what Mulally did—assess the overall situation, analyze how the company is failing, set out a plan to retool your mission statement, then use that statement to help you focus on achieving success. This means asking yourself a series of questions. What does your company stand for? What services do you want to provide? How will you stand out from the competition? For Mulally, the answer was to sell off pieces of the company that did not fit with its core values. What do you need to do to make your goal more focused and on target?

Once you have a clear vision, you need to make sure that all parts of your organization work in support of that vision. Motivate your staff by creating a culture that embraces the goals of your mission statement. "Consistency is key when trying to achieve a goal," Mulally stressed to me. I've seen things as simple as a sign transcribing the mission statement on the bulletin board of a break room or inspirational Post-it notes in employee cubicles. In order to achieve success at this level of the pyramid, every member of the team needs to fully support the goal. Mulally told me if his employees did not share this vision, they left. It's not that they weren't performing; they just didn't have the commitment or passion the company was looking for.

Like Mulally, you need to truly believe in your mission. It can't just be some pretty verbiage in a nice frame. If you don't truly believe in what you are trying to achieve why would you expect your employees to believe? Remember, you are the ultimate example.

**If you are an employee:**

Look within yourself and ask what talents you bring to your organization. What can you contribute? If you have ideas, write them down and ask your boss if you can share them with him or her. Look at the competition. Are they showing any weaknesses that could open the door of opportunity for your organization to expand its footprint? Are there inefficiencies that can be addressed? Mulally's advice on the path to innovation is something all employees can internalize: "You never want an improvement to pass you by, because you need that improvement every month, every year, in order to continue on your path to continuously improve and deliver that compelling vision."

Finally, remember that Mulally and leaders like him want employees who are engaged. Are you engaged? Your actions speak louder than your words. How would you honestly rate your productivity and your efforts toward achieving your organization's goals?

**If you are an aspiring entrepreneur:**

Starting a business can be a challenge, but a mission statement helps you focus on your growth plans and which opportunities to take. You need your goals spelled out. Then you need to list how you will achieve them. Mulally will be the first to tell you it isn't easy. You need to take action. "You don't wait for an opportunity," he says. "It doesn't come to you when you are just sitting in a room."

It's true that in order to take advantage of opportunity, you need money, and when you're a budding entrepreneur capital is probably tight. That is why it is so important to have a mission statement. It will be your true north and keep you on task.

---

## FINAL THOUGHTS

Mulally's story is a great example of how a mission statement provides you with both focus and stability in leading. Not only does this level of the pyramid help you define your goals and solidify your foundation, it nurtures and ignites the next level of the pyramid: passion.

# 5                          Fuel Your Passion

**Steve Case**

I T DOESN'T MATTER if you are a baker, banker, stay-at-home mom, employee, or even a kid with an idea—if you're not passionate, you're not going anywhere. Passion is the fuel that keeps you going, wondering, testing yourself. I have never met a successful businessperson or entrepreneur who was not passionate. Some have infectious, larger-than-life personalities, while others are so low-key they fly under the radar. But they all share one thing: the burning desire to strive and do their best.

I remember one of the first times I met someone who embodied this trait. I was working at WFTV in Orlando as the nightside assignment editor and there was a reporter I admired: Jane Watrel. Anytime she walked in, her passion and energy filled up the room. She always came with a story, an angle, and always pushed and questioned. Those qualities were a product of her love of reporting.

When I think of passion, another person who immediately comes to mind is Steve Case, best known as cofounder and former chief executive of America Online. Since retiring as chairman of AOL–Time Warner in 2003, Case has invested in more than 30 startups in the United States through his company Revolution, not to mention mentoring hundreds more startups around the country.

Case has experienced the heights of success and the depths of failure, yet his passion has never waned. Undeterred by personal tragedy and business hardships, Case continues to mentor, advise, and invest in the next wave of innovative companies seeking to change the world. A few examples of his triple threat of investing, mentoring, and advising include Zipcar, LivingSocial, and Lolly Wolly Doodle.

In his roles as chairman of President Obama's Startup America Partnership and member of the President's Council on Jobs and Competitiveness, Case tries to make the voices of entrepreneurs heard in the DC Beltway. He also uses social media daily to stress the need for political reform to help business thrive—at the time of this writing, he was working on helping to pass immigration reform. (I am one of his 600,000-plus followers on Twitter. He is on my Twitter deck in my "influencers" list.)

## REVOLUTION CALLING

Passion can start a revolution. It drives you to rise above. It energizes you to push for change. Case's "revolution" started at the age of 10 while living in paradise: Honolulu, Hawaii. "Growing up on an island is a bit different than most childhood experiences, but I really enjoyed it," he says. "I had the entrepreneurial itch from an early age. I was always starting little businesses, whether it was setting up a juice stand with my brother, or selling greeting cards and newspapers door-to-door."
Case's partner was his older brother Dan, the financier behind Case's childhood business endeavors. He has affectionately recalled his ventures: "Other kids played tag. We played business. I would go broke, and he would bail me out."

Although growing up in Hawaii was a wonderful experience, it wasn't enough to satisfy his insatiable entrepreneurial appetite. Case went to Williams College in Massachusetts, his father's alma mater. He would not go on to follow in his father's career footsteps. He explains, "My father and brothers were lawyers, so most people probably thought I'd do that too. But I was always fascinated by business and the opportunity to build things."

Being in college didn't stop Case from starting ventures. One of his creations was a fruit-basket company targeting parents of college students who wanted to send goodies to their kids. The real ah-ha moment came when he was a senior. "I read a book by the futurist Alvin Toffler called *The Third Wave*," he recalls. "He talked about a futuristic, connected world. This idea of an 'electronic cottage'—what would become the Internet—captivated me. I was certain that the day would arrive, as

Toffler described, when we harnessed technology to build a whole new medium for communications, commerce, news, and entertainment. Of course, there were no Internet companies to work for when I graduated from Williams College—none existed—so I initially followed a more traditional post-college career path, but ... I knew I wanted to set out to play a role building this new medium, and it was only a matter of time before I found a way to do it: cofounding AOL."

Case's "traditional path" took him to Procter & Gamble after he graduated from Williams in 1980. After that, he was off to PepsiCo's Pizza Hut division in Kansas. "I learned a lot in both roles, but knew I wouldn't be satisfied staying on a big-company path," Case told me. "I didn't want to *manage* brands that been around for decades, I wanted to *lead* in the development of new brands and new businesses."

Little did he know an opportunity was just around the corner. In 1983, his brother Dan invested in a startup called Control Video Corporation through the Hambrecht & Quist venture-capital fund. Control Video was a company that turned Atari VCS video game machines into interactive devices using a product called GameLine. At the annual electronics show that year, Dan introduced Steve to the company's current head, William von Meister. When he was asked to join, Case knew the time to lead a new brand was now. "I jumped at it," he says. "I knew it was risky, but felt staying where I was to be even riskier, as my passion was around entrepreneurship, and in particular about playing a role in pioneering the creation of the new interactive medium."

Pretty sure this would be "the next big thing," Case quit his safe and dependable job with the Fortune 500 company, packed up all his belongings in his car, and drove to Virginia to join Control Video. But the dream of being part of a technical disrupter quickly turned into a nightmare. He recalls, "At my first board meeting, one of Control Video's investors looked at the weak sales and quipped: 'You'd have thought they would have shoplifted more than that.' The company was collapsing."

You know the old saying: when one door closes, another opens? That was how Case and some of his colleagues chose to view the closing of Control Video. In 1985, Case and a few of his team members started a new company called Quantum Computer Services, which ultimately became America Online. He says, "We were taking lessons learned from our GameLine experiences and focusing on PCs instead of video game machines. We learned the hard lesson about bringing a product to market in a consumer world where it's very expensive to build a brand and get distribution and so forth, so we decided to partner with PC companies and use their brands and have them take the lead *and* spend the money. I think it's safe to say that without the failure of GameLine, there would have never been the success of America Online."

## SUCCESS BORN OUT OF FAILURE

Let's be honest, no one can really predict the future. There may be signs of things to come, but sometimes we are blinded by our passion to succeed. It is a powerful force within us. We need to learn to keep our eyes open, and, if we make mistakes, learn from them. Case is no different from you or me in this respect. "In retrospect, the company [Control Video] made a lot of mistakes," he explains as he looks back, "but out of those mistakes, and that failure, I learned a great deal about what to do, and what *not* to do. Those lessons helped teach me how to start a company, how to grow a team, how to build partnerships, and much more. I believed so passionately in the promise of a new interactive medium that I wasn't ready to give up just yet. So I said, 'Well, let's figure out another way to come at this.'"

Case could have tucked his tail between his legs and gone back to corporate life, but he didn't. Instead, he and the former GameLine crew figured out the way to tap into the consumer by partnering with PC companies, leveraging the PC brand names and money in order to create the online community they were striving to build. They saw something and learned how to achieve success through experiencing failure. It doesn't matter if you are an entrepreneur like Case or you are working your way up the corporate ladder—passion and fearlessness are two key ingredients to success. Success *can* be born out of failure. Leaders face adversity head on—they know what they're up against and acknowledge their strengths and weaknesses.

## BUILDING UP FROM PASSION

When asked to describe the journey of entrepreneurship, Case was thoughtful and reflective: "It is a long and difficult road—there are ups and downs, moments of glory and moments of despair," he says. "To be a successful entrepreneur leading a team through such uncertainty, inner passion is a necessity. You have to believe in the objective—and care enough, with every fiber in your body—that you will weather the hard times in order to get to a new day."

When Case and his colleagues started AOL in 1985, it was certainly not an overnight success. "There were many ups and downs along the road—several painful layoffs in the first few years. We were a niche player in what at the time was a tiny market—when we started AOL, only 3 percent of people were online, and we had a tiny share of that tiny market. Without a strong passion for our mission—to build a new medium that could change the world and to get America online—our success would never have been realized," he says.

One of the most important things Case says he learned is that regardless of the type of issue—whether it's product development, branding, or sales—the common denominator is invariably the people who make up the organization. Success or failure depends on the individuals involved. "If you have a talented group of people that are passionate and well led, I don't think there's a limit on what can be achieved in terms of building a great organization or a great brand," he says. "At AOL it took us nearly a decade to get one million subscribers to AOL, and then in the next decade we went from one million to more than 25 million. Our challenge back then was getting people to believe in the Internet, to crack the myth of it as a marvel of science fiction and approach it instead as a functional tool for communicating and accessing content of all sorts. That's why we emphasized ease of use and created a portal that was intuitive for people. We apply many of those same lessons today when advising our portfolio companies."

## DEFINING MOMENTS

Every leader has a moment when their company either rises to the occasion or fails. Case recalls that the "transformational moment" for AOL came out of what could have been considered a corporate catastrophe. "I had camped out in Cupertino for six months and convinced Apple to partner with us to launch the AppleLink Personal Edition service. But soon after signing the contract we began to run into a clash of perspectives, ultimately boiling down to our belief that the software service should be given away for free, and we parted ways," he explains. "That led to the launch of the AOL brand. We held an internal contest to rename AppleLink and the best entry was 'Online America.'"

Case says that since the company had no money to spend on marketing, it needed a descriptive name that would "sell itself." At the last minute, they decided "America Online" sounded better than "Online America," so they flipped the words and rebranded AppleLink as America Online in 1989. By 1990, the team's sole focus was America Online. "Within weeks, the users started calling it 'AO' and 'AOL.' We decided to embrace 'AOL' and that became the brand we rallied around. In retrospect, while Apple pulling the plug on AppleLink was a crisis at the time—indeed, it could have been a catastrophe—ultimately it turned out to be the best thing that ever happened to us."

A company can be defined by both positive and negative moments, as was soon demonstrated by AOL's merger with Time Warner. During the Internet boom, AOL was riding high—indeed, it was the most successful company of the 1990s. In 1999, advisers within AOL decided the "perfect" merger would be with Time Warner. AOL advisers, along with Wall Street, had a vision of blending news, entertainment, television and music content with online communications. To this day, the AOL–Time Warner merger remains the largest merger in the history of US business.[7] Case became chairman of the newly joined company. "It was a smart deal for AOL shareholders," explains Case. "They traded 100 percent of a company with $5 billion in revenue and a billion dollars in profit for 55 percent of the newly combined company with $40 billion in revenue and $10 billion in profit." (Case also had a dream for AOL to acquire the then-struggling Apple Computer, but there was no interest. As I type this book on my iPad, I wonder what would have happened if Case did succeed.)

Although the merger looked like a great idea on paper, one of the biggest hurdles (pointed out by many on Wall Street and in the media) was combining the two companies' very different cultures. Cultures are born from and nurtured by the beliefs and values shared by a company's workers. The ways in which a company addresses opportunity and adversity are based in culture. When the merger happened, there was the buttoned-down corporate culture of Time Warner on the one hand, and the entrepreneurial spirit of AOL on the other. The deal forged in January 2001 was later dubbed "the worst deal in history," and one of the reasons it didn't work was that these two cultures clashed.[8]

Timing didn't help, either—the Internet bubble exploded, and Time Warner stock, had which sold for $90 a share at the time of the merger announcement, sank to a mere $12 a share a few months later as AOL–Time Warner stock. The synergies promised never came to fruition, and advertising revenue failed to meet expectations. In 2003, there was a management shakeup, and Case, along with other AOL executives, parted ways with the company he built. While Case admitted later in a 2006 interview with Charlie Rose he "was sorry" about the execution of the merger, it didn't stop him from moving on.[9]

As if this challenging chapter in his life wasn't enough for Case, he was also facing a personal crisis. It was a crisis that would forever shape his path in business and lead him to where he is today. Case's brother, Dan, was diagnosed with a brain tumor in 2001. In helping Dan, Case saw firsthand the maze of redundant, complicated paperwork that patients in this terrifying situation had to fill out, the frustration that goes along with the breakdown in communication in the health care system, and the emotional *why* questions that go unanswered, leaving frustration and despair. Why was information so hard to come by? Why were some of the treatments so inadequate? What treatments are available? How do you qualify? Why did it take so long to get test results? The quest for information was daunting, and Case had had enough. To help answer these questions, he founded a nonprofit, Accelerate Brain Cancer Cure, in 2001. Then in 2005, he formed Revolution Health Group—a version of America Online with an online community devoted 100 percent to health care. Information from top centers like the Mayo Clinic and help for insurance issues were all included.

Tragically, Dan succumbed to his illness a little more than a year after he was diagnosed. Have you ever had a pivotal moment like that? These defining moments can either crush you or build you up. Case could have chosen to let the tragedy of his brother's death or the failure of the AOL–Time Warner merger be his downfall. He could have given up. But he didn't let losing his brother or the failed merger define him. Instead he used his experiences as stepping stones. He was empowered to do something about what had happened and refused to be labeled.

Personally, I like to prove people wrong. If someone doubts me, it drives me to succeed even more. I smile at my naysayers—as my papa once told me, "Kill them with kindness." Sometimes people are negative because they have low self-esteem and are threatened by the mere possibility of your success. These are the people who try to tear you down to their level. That's why it is so important to surround yourself with positive people. You don't want negativity to snuff out your passion.

## LOOKING BEYOND THE BIG PICTURE

For good leaders, opportunity is *always* on the horizon. They focus through the windshield—never the rear-view mirror—and realize there are different ways to measure an opportunity.

Let me give you an example. I measure opportunity through lists. Whenever I'm exploring an opportunity in front of me, I make a list of the pros and cons. I follow that with a list of my strengths and weaknesses as they apply to that particular opportunity. I ask, What do *I* bring to the opportunity in front of me? What sets me apart? What will this opportunity *provide* me?

When I started in the news industry, I freelanced behind the scenes at a cable outlet near my hometown. I was hired after an internship there and it was my first job. While it was great to be working near family and friends, I yearned for more. I wanted to be a reporter. I loved covering stories in the field. That passion drove me to create my own opportunity.

While attending a sorority sister's wedding I became acquainted with Watertown, a small town in upstate New York near the Fort Drum US Army reservation. I thought the town was great. My sorority sister told me there was a television station there, so I researched the station and contacted the news director for an informational interview. The interview went well, and the news director told me that if they had any openings they would call me. A week later, I was offered a part-time job as a photojournalist and reporter. It would be a combination of shooting stories for other reporters, editing the stories for air, running the studio camera during the newscast, and reporting on my own stories.

I immediately made a list. The pros were obvious. This opportunity gave me a chance to report. The cons? Carrying 30 pounds of gear in bad weather conditions (blizzards, pouring rain, floods, and sweltering heat) and editing under intense deadlines. Then there was operating a studio camera during a live newscast, something I did in college that I didn't enjoy, nor did I want to pursue a career in it—it just wasn't for me.

The cons outweighed the pros, but reporting was what I wanted to do. I knew if I did a great job, doors would open. I also knew the experience of learning the other jobs would help me appreciate all sides of the news-gathering process and would make me be a better team player. I would understand and be able to relate to what my other colleagues behind the scenes were trying to achieve. Besides, even a "dream job" has some downsides. You're fooling yourself if think otherwise. I was filled to the brim with passion and jumped at the opportunity. I filled a U-Haul and moved.

I never regretted that decision. I evolved as a videographer. My defining moment in television journalism came when my video of the 10th Mountain Division deployment to Haiti was on *CBS News* with Dan Rather. I was 22 at the time, and I was the first photojournalist to capture video of the early morning deployment. Seeing the video I shot and edited on national television was a moment I'll never forget. Moreover, that job gave me the tools I still use to this day. My shooting experience helps me when I field produce interviews as well as sit in edit sessions. It helped me produce a documentary. I can communicate better with my videographer and editor because I have performed their jobs, so I understand how they are analyzing and approaching a story.

When Case defines opportunity, he looks beyond the here-and-now and focuses on how it can be a step toward his future. He looks at the whole picture plus some: "To me an opportunity means there is a better way to do something and entrepreneurs recognize that and seize the day to capitalize on the opportunities they are particularly passionate about. It's like waiting for the right pitch, and when it comes, going for it and swinging for the fences."

Case may not make pro-and-con lists like I do, but he does have a checklist he firmly stands by when exploring an opportunity:

- **Have a big idea:** "We like ideas that matter, because the resulting products and services can improve people's lives. We like ideas that can become big businesses. Indeed, our investing strategy at Revolution is to identify the entrepreneurs with the big ideas when they are still small companies, and work with them to capitalize on the opportunity and build a successful business."

- **Build it to last:** "While some entrepreneurs start out with the goal of building a built-to-flip company—that is, a business that starts up quickly and is sold off to a bigger corporation—we seek to find the opposite. We want entrepreneurs who take the long view, and are building a disruptive business that will stand the test of time, and hopefully change the world. There is nothing wrong with built-to-flip, but our passion is helping to build iconic, built-to-last businesses."

- **Invest in people:** "Ideas matter, but people are equally important. The team matters a great deal. We invest in people and ideas that can change the world. We do that both through our nonprofit efforts at the Case Foundation, and through our for-profit investments at Revolution. We focus on a number of companies on the for-profit side that are attacking a significant market that is ripe for disruption. These opportunities may take five or ten years to come to fruition. A great example is Zipcar—the car-sharing service that has revolutionized travel in urban areas."

Case's three points deliver the same endgame as my lists of pros and cons. He references this list again and again when exploring opportunities. What do you do when you are presented with an opportunity? How do you think big?

## INTUITION VS. EDUCATION

Case, a "B" student by his own admission, believes you need a mix of formal education and real-world education to succeed. He emphasizes leading with passion and intuition: "Bill Gates, Steve Jobs, Richard Branson, Mark Zuckerberg, and Michael Dell were all pioneering founders who did not have college degrees, yet they built great entrepreneurial companies. So obviously a college degree is not essential. But I think it is helpful, as it gives you perspectives that likely will help down the road. I'm less sure a graduate degree is necessary, or even helpful, for entrepreneurs. It's critical if you want to be a manager in a large company but not as needed if you want to be an entrepreneur building a start-up." This statement can be applied to any industry. Remember, Harold Hamm didn't have a formal college education, either.

Along his entrepreneurial journey, Case did apply to business school, but it was when he was right out of college, and he was rejected. They prefer people—as they should, he says—who have work experience. However, he reflects: "In retrospect I'm glad I didn't go. I think I would have ended up focusing more on analyzing and minimizing risk, and the paths I've chosen to pursue instead require intuition and the ability to maximize opportunity."

## THREE P'S

Case also maximizes opportunity through his team. It doesn't matter whom I speak with—all CEOs tell me human capital is the key to success. Case would agree with Alan Mulally that culture is key. "In all of my business endeavors I have made it a point to hire the most talented and passionate people. Surrounding yourself and your company with talent is essential to grow. You can't do it alone," he stresses. "Indeed, there's an African proverb that says if you want to go quickly, go alone, but if you want to go far, you must go together. I like big ideas that take some time to develop, and can be developed only by a team. Entrepreneurs must be talent scouts all the time, always on the lookout for people to add to their team." Case explains the "three Ps" they live by at Revolution: **p**eople, **p**assion, and **p**erseverance. "With those three things coupled together, almost anything can happen. Without them, not much can happen," he says.

Case emphasizes that his company's financial investment only goes so far. It's the "people" aspect—the experience they bring to the table and the way they nurture relationships—that is the key to success for these companies. Passion is just as important as the money, if not more. "You need to have passion for the mission," he says. "You have to believe—and care enough, with every fiber in your body—so you can weather the hard times in order to get to a better place. If you are in it for any reason other than passion, it's hard to be a successful entrepreneur."

## PAYING IT FORWARD

From forming his own foundation to being part of the Giving Pledge—a commitment by the world's wealthiest individuals, including Case, Warren Buffet, Bill Gates, and others, to dedicate the majority of their wealth to philanthropy—Case is about paying forward. "It's incredibly gratifying to give advice to entrepreneurs. In fact, I can think of few things more gratifying than helping someone bring their idea to life and achieve their dream," he says. "I see it as the responsibility of every successful entrepreneur to act as a mentor and coach for the next generation of entrepreneurs."

Helping aspiring entrepreneurs is part of how Case stokes his inner passion. "Engaging and spending time with entrepreneurs inspires me each day. The story of America is the story of entrepreneurs. Yes, the patriots created the republic and built the democracy, but it is the *entrepreneurs* who innovated and built our economy. And that in turn is why America is the leader of the free world," he told me. "That is why I devote time to advocating on behalf of entrepreneurs—whether as an investor in specific businesses, a cheerleader for a specific region, or as an advocate for pro-entrepreneurship policies with governments."

Since leaving AOL more than a decade ago, Case has had the opportunity to invest in and help build more than a dozen companies. Like a proud papa, Case roots for their successes: "Today, I find nothing more gratifying than watching and helping an entrepreneur come up with an idea, build a team, go for it, and ultimately succeed. To me, the story and promise of America is retold with each successful entrepreneurial venture."

## BUILDING YOUR PYRAMID

Case's passion is unstoppable. If you want to enjoy his level of success, you need to have that same level of passion, whether you're running your own company or someone else's. Of the hundreds of CEOs I have spoken with, all agree that the spark needs to come from within—you can't learn it, you can't delegate it, you can't fake it. I've come to know some of the world's most successful business titans, and like Steve Case, they all have a deep passion for what they do.

But Case's story also shows that it takes time to grow a business. It's hard sometimes when you have the fire burning in your belly and you just want to jump in and go Mach 10. But you need to remember to be sure your objectives are clear and the steps you are taking will lead you to your ultimate goal. Passion is raw emotion. Passion can be blinding. There are no shortcuts to success. It's a delicate balance between harnessing your passion, going down your checklist, prioritizing your spending, and valuing your human capital. All of these elements need to be blended together. You need to figure out a way to balance between your drive to succeed and driving people away.

A Page from My Notebook: **Steve Case**

### Rules to Live By

- Dream big—embrace bold, swing-for-the-fences, change-the-world ideas.
- Recruit constantly—you can't do it on your own, so you must hire great people and build a great team to do great things.
- Embrace risk—it's a critical part of the entrepreneurial journey, so take risks, and be innovative.

### Mantra

Be fearless.

### Life Lessons

- Be curious. Be open. Be flexible. Let your life unfold as a series of chapters.
- As Wayne Gretzky once said, "Don't focus on where the puck is... focus on where it is going."
- "Vision without execution is hallucination," said Thomas Edison. Inspiration matters, but execution matters more.
- This African proverb on the need for teams: "If you want to go quickly, go alone. If you want to go far, go together."

Here are tips on how to apply Case's story:

## If you are a business owner or manager:

Case's story should show you that no matter how little money you have to start your business, you can make a go of it. Look for creative ways of marketing, as Case did by creating a company name that "sold itself."

In order to achieve Case's level of marketing prowess, you can't forget the criteria he used, and still uses to this day, when assessing a potential opportunity. These three criteria are critical:

- Have a big idea.
- Look for platform opportunities, not just product opportunities.
- Invest in people who can change the world.

Remember what Case says about big ideas that take time to develop. His businesses were not created overnight; they took many years. Patience is vital for business owners and managers. Recall that one of the key ingredients in Case's growth plan was putting together a good team. This takes time. Synergies need to develop for a cohesive unit to emerge.

One of the ways to stoke your employees' passion is to show them you trust them. Delegation is important. How would you grade your delegation of duties? Those of us who are "Type A" tend to want to do it all, but there comes a point where you need to rely on others. It doesn't mean you are weak. Remember that delegation doesn't mean leaving people on their own completely. You can create a system of checks and balances to make sure everything is being done to your standards.

Ultimately, that bar is set and enforced through strong leadership. You need to provide the vision, guidance, and example of how to achieve the goals set out. Keeping on task and on budget helps strengthen this level of the opportunity pyramid.

## If you are an employee:

Even if you're not in a management position, you can still inspire others. If you work hard and show confidence, your talent will be recognized and you can be given opportunities you never thought were possible. Remember, leaders are looking for the next generation to help the company grow. Case would be the first to tell you it's the people in the company who add value and growth potential, whether the organization is Zipcar, AOL, or the children's clothing company Lolly Wolly Doodle.

If you have ideas for cutting costs or expanding your company's brand, sit down and thoughtfully go over them, and then ask to present them to your boss. Even if your ideas are not adopted, they show initiative. Maybe they will even inspire you to start you own company! You also need to keep your eagerness in check. Plans often take time to be adopted and executed. Showing patience and understanding goes a long way.

### If you are an aspiring entrepreneur:

Recall Case's advice that "If you are in it for any reason other than passion, it's hard to be a successful entrepreneur." I have seen small business owners and CEOs who have lacked that passion, and it doesn't take too long before the business suffers. Do you want it bad enough? Are you consumed by what you want to do? That's the drive Case is talking about. It's this type of drive that will comfort as well as energize you as you approach the next level of the pyramid. It's your sustenance.

---

## FINAL THOUGHTS

One of the most important lessons of Case's career is to learn from both your successes and your failures. His passion did not make him impulsive, but rather steered him through the difficult times and sharpened his focus. As you build each layer of your opportunity pyramid there will be risks to take, but just remember what Case stressed—be sure they go back to the passion at your essence, which defines what you are trying to achieve. This anonymous quote sums it up: "20 years from now you will be more disappointed by the things you didn't do than by the ones you did. So throw off the bowlines. Sail away from the safe harbor. Catch the trade winds in your sails. Explore. Dream. Discover."

# 6                                    Stay the Course

## Ron Kruszewski

I F BEING PASSIONATE is like catching the wind in your sails, the next level of the pyramid could be compared to following a lighthouse in the distance. Staying true to yourself and blocking out the noise that could cause you to veer off course are key at this level of the pyramid. Ron Kruszewski, one of the most successful CEOs on Wall Street, embraces this ideology.

Kruszewski is chairman and CEO of Stifel Financial Corp. His track record speaks for itself: in 2005 his company's revenue was $250 million and its market cap was $200 million. Today, revenue is $2 billion with a market cap of $2.5 billion.[10] By never straying from his beacon of light—and staying true to his opportunity execution plan—Kruszewski beat the odds.

Stifel's financial record is a testament to Ron's consistent leadership. Kruszewski was 38 when he took the job at Stifel in 1997. Under his control, the company's stock price has increased by more than 820 percent, which is impressive compared to a group of peers that the company tracks, whose stocks have returned an average of 38 percent over the same period. In the last decade, that same peer group returned a negative 8.9 percent compared to Stifel's 690 percent increase. Stifel's net revenues have increased over $1.3 billion during the last decade, from $187 million in 2002 to almost $1.5 billion through the 12 months that ended June 30, 2012. Importantly, core earnings have also increased over the same period from $4.7 million to $110 million, an increase of 2,199 percent.[11]

By staying grounded in conservative values, Kruszewski avoided the excessive leverage that hurt many firms during the financial crisis. He has instead preferred to keep a strong capital base so that the firm can be in a position to take advantage of opportunities. Stifel's total assets are about $8.5 billion today and are supported by an equity capital base of approximately $1.9 billion.[12]

Since Kruszewski's debut in the C-suite, the company has blazed an acquisitions trail, buying Legg Mason Capital Management, Ryan Beck & Co., 56 branches of UBS Wealth Management Americas, Thomas Weisel Partners, and Stone & Youngberg. Stifel also made a $30 million investment in competitor Knight Capital Group. In 2010, Stifel was named one of the top five fastest-growing financial services businesses by *Fortune*, and it shows no signs of slowing down.[13]

But Kruszewski is not just buying whatever financial services firm he sees next. He has a discerning eye, and his risk and quality criteria have to be met. The bottom line for this CEO is being nimble and selective when assessing opportunity. A charismatic CEO with a big warm smile, Kruszewski told me people have always said he is lucky, but he likes to tell them: "I was prepared for the opportunity when it presented itself. My basic business plan is to be prepared and take advantage of opportunities when they present themselves. You get ready for opportunity by preparing your organization to get ready for change. It's all about embracing action."

## CULTURE CREATION

I have met hundreds of very successful business leaders during the course of my career as a producer and author, and regardless of the industry they are in, they all have a positive business culture that started at—and was embraced from—the top. As with Mulally and Case, culture is a central focus for Kruszewski, and part of his company's culture is an open mindset: "I have never told my employees that I know everything. I don't, and I'm open to change. Our organization today is the melding of many deals. We are one firm today, but we are the best because of all the different firms that make up Stifel. Your infrastructure has to be prepared. That's the bottom line."

Kruszewski did not hesitate when describing his endgame: "I always say I want to be able to double the firm tomorrow if I have to. And that's how I approach my business. I have the people and the plan to be able to increase the firm very quickly in terms of our capability; I just don't know when it's going to take place. If you set the right culture and thought process, growing a company with people who are nimble and thrive on change is self-selecting."

## THE POWER OF LISTENING

One of the greatest talents businesspeople can possess is the ability to listen and to then act on what they've heard. All too often, leaders do all the talking in conversations with employees and, as a result, nothing happens. This creates a feeling among employees that their input doesn't matter and that change will never happen. From day one, Kruszewski didn't want to be that guy. He told me, "It was Monday, September 29, 1997. I promised my wife that I would listen, because back then I was a terrible listener. I went to an executive committee meeting at Stifel Financial, and there were twelve people in the meeting. It went from nine to noon. What fascinated me about the meeting was the number of problems that were discussed around the table, like the email guy saying the email system didn't work, and the sales guy giving him advice on how to fix it. For those three hours, people just talked and talked about problems. But what struck me the most about this meeting was there were no solutions being offered. It was a classic committee hearing. So after the three hours, I asked the group how often they met, and they told me they met every Monday, Wednesday, and Friday from nine until noon. I said, 'Really?,' and I left. Well, I went home and I told my wife I was going to break my rule and say something at the next meeting."

What Ron proceeded to do amazed his colleagues and set a new precedent. Wanting to let committee members know he heard them, he said, "I want to adjourn the meeting right now. I want you all to go back and fix the problems you are all talking about. And then, after that, I want you to identify more problems and fix those. I will send you all an email—that's if our email system is up and running—telling you all when our next executive committee meeting will be." He remembers: "That was October 1, 1997. I have never sent an email to call for another executive committee meeting. In fact, we don't even have an executive committee anymore." By listening to his employees, Kruszewski was able to see the culture of Stifel at work firsthand, and to understand its glaring weaknesses. By "breaking his rule," he empowered his workers to fix what was broken.

What makes Kruszewski a successful leader is this immediate, often-informal style of communication. It enables him and his team to stay the course. "The bureaucratic aspect of management is not something we embrace here. If you like that and that is how you are trained, you will not survive here and you won't like it. I've lost very good and talented people because of that," he says. By design, he has created a management team he describes as nimble: "They are client facing; we don't spend a lot of time planning. Now you're probably saying, 'How can you run an organization like that?' But it ends up being very nimble and entrepreneurial." Because the organization doesn't get caught up in bureaucratic minutia, it is able to stay on task and continuously move forward.

## FIVE-YEAR PLAN SMACKDOWN

When I asked Kruszewski how he defines opportunity, he said that providing a definition would go against his business philosophy: "If I could define opportunity, I would be missing the point, because I am never quite sure where the opportunity is coming from. If I did define opportunity, that would mean I have to make a plan. In fact, it's the opposite. Opportunity presents itself to you. You are never sure where it is going to come from. The hallmark of opportunity is that you are out there with a plan saying you are going to do a specific thing, and you look for just that opportunity and execute on that. That's not taking advantage of opportunity."

For every 50 opportunities Kruszewski says he is presented with, he may take advantage of one. He uses three criteria to judge opportunities:

- The opportunity has to be a good "people" fit. Kruszewski explains: "In my business, the 'assets' are the people, and therefore the strategic fit [is] the people."
- The opportunity would have to create shareholder value in a fair, reasonable timeframe.
- The opportunity would have to add to the organization's existing capabilities.

After analyzing the possible opportunity against this list, Kruszewski considers one final criterion: the quality of the opportunity, independent of how much growth it would create. "I live by this," he says. "We are not interested in taking advantage of opportunity just to get bigger. We're not interested in setting out to be the number-one issuer of IPOs, because if you do that, by definition, you will sacrifice quality. The game there is quantity. Being bigger does not necessarily mean better."

"I spend my life evaluating opportunity," he continues. "I don't spend my life trying to create an opportunity. That is a very important distinction. It is a difference between believing a business plan is 'to do' something, versus letting opportunity come to you. This is something many people don't understand. You are taught in business school that you should define your opportunities and define your markets. But I don't think anyone can really do that. Bad deals are born out of strategic planning. Boards will approve a 'strategic plan,' management will then have a set goal, compensation will then be based on success of that strategic plan, and management will continue fulfilling that plan, even if it is not in the best interest of shareholders, because of the compensation tied to the deal."

Since you can't predict the future, how can you predict you'll make a specific number of deals within a specific timeframe? Kruszewski explains that his deals with Legg Mason Capital Management, Ryan Beck, and UBS Wealth Management Americas were deals he did not think they would do: "Even our acquisition of Thomas Weisel Partners was one that presented itself to us. We didn't set out to acquire X amount of firms." This is why he feels the "five-year plan" many organizations swear by can actually steer you away from opportunity: "If that opportunity is not a part of your 'five-year plan,' you will disregard it."

## LAZY LIKE A FOX

Kruszewski's unconventional way of leading faced some serious headwinds from his board at first, but that didn't influence his leadership strategy. He admits, "For years my board yelled at me for not giving them a strategic plan. They thought I was lazy. They would want to go on strategic planning retreats. I said, we can go play golf, but we are not going to do strategic planning. That was difficult for them to accept for a while. But when you look at our growth, strategic planning would have never been able to identify the opportunities we seized on. It was an interesting transformation of our board. After our fifth deal, they caught on and understood my business strategy."

At the end of the day, success or failure is based on results, not planning. "I show my board last year's cost structure, and we compare the present revenues and costs year over year," Kruszewski says. "If the revenues of the year are up 15 percent, we go out and celebrate; if we are down 15 percent, we don't." They focus on discussing and planning what they would do if revenues were down 15 percent: "We never predict revenues will be up 15 percent. How can you possibly plan in our industry? We are tied directly to the capital markets. It's a fool's game to predict." In order to be prepared for a downturn, though, Kruszewski has risk committees who have created parameters.

His organization chart is a perfect example of his focus on results over processes. In 1997, Stifel was the first firm to "flip" the organization chart. The chart has Kruszewski at the bottom and the people who serve clients at the top. "When banks grow, what do they do? They build the biggest building in town, and they put their executives at the top floor. No client can get onto that floor. So the financial services sector hierarchy is built that way," he explains. His company's client-oriented structure helps them stay focused and on course, and its results speak for themselves.

Kruszewski's unconventional organizational structure is also connected to the entrepreneurial nature of his business. He told me, "Business schools teach you that a formation of a business is a triangle, where the point at the top is your entry into the marketplace. Think of the point as a Nordstrom or McDonald's store. Business schools will teach you marketing and branding. That works if you are selling hamburgers or clothes. No matter where you go, every McDonald's is the same. But when it comes to financial services, we interact with thousands of people, and the product has to be entrepreneurial in order to meet the financial needs of customers. That structure does not fit our business. Turning the chart upside down has had a direct impact on our stock price." As shown in the chart comparing Stifel to the other companies in the sector (see page 83), Stifel was up 821 percent for the period between October 1997 and September 2012. The next-best firm, Raymond James, was up 100 percent for the decade. "We trounce them," he said with a smile. "We did this because we didn't have a strategic plan. We didn't do something [just] because it sounded good on paper. I don't give guidance to the Street. Nothing. How can I give guidance if I don't know where the next opportunity may present itself?"

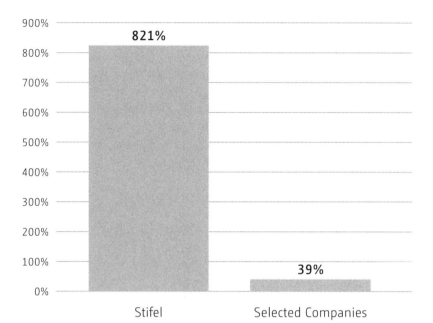

## ABSOLUTE APPRECIATION/(DEPRECIATION), STIFEL VS. SELECTED COMPANIES 10/1/1997–9/30/2012

Source: Stifel Financial Corp.

### AVOIDING PLANNING PARALYSIS

Organizations often become paralyzed by the process of planning. There's an old joke: "My whole day is in meetings; there's no time to do my job." By trying to do everything "by the book," organizations miss the potential opportunity of taking a risk. Kruszewski's method of anticipating problems stands in contrast to planning for planning's sake alone. "I ask my senior staff all the time to think about what events could cause problems that no one is thinking about. Good leaders are always thinking, evaluating," he says.

With conviction in his voice, he asked, "How can a spreadsheet identify opportunity? There are no bullet points or instructions on how to live your life. The same should apply to running a business and capturing opportunity. Unlike most business executives who start their year with a defined strategic plan, my strategic plan is defined as you go by the opportunities that present themselves during the year."

This management style is only effective, however, if you keep a firm grasp on the numbers and where they may be leading you. Kruszewski may be laissez-faire as it relates to planning and organizational structure, but he describes a rigidity in himself from which he derives his everyday business model: "I am a student of the numbers. If those numbers go adrift, I deal with it. I am versed in all of our business models as well or better than the people running the businesses. I believe in letting the future come to you. Once your opportunities come to you and you corral them and you are stable, I believe you need to be very strict on the business models, expense controls, and running the business in order to successfully grow your business."

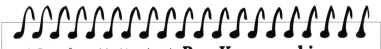

A Page from My Notebook: **Ron Kruszewski**

---

### Rules to Live By

- I jealously guard how I use my time. There is no greater resource to me than my time. I endeavor to make sure that I am working off my to-do list rather than reacting to the priorities of others. This requires some flexibility, of course, but I make a daily listing of my personal priorities and fit them into my available time.
- I make career goals that are general and directional. As opportunities have come my way, I evaluate whether this new opportunity—even within my current organization—is consistent with my long-term goals.
- I am a consummate "brain picker." I try to find the best minds in a field, and I try to learn from them. Most people are very willing to mentor and help others who are sincerely interested in their field. Also, I try to remember this lesson when people ask me to be a mentor.

- I try to be respectful. Every person, regardless of status or stature, is entitled to be treated respectfully—until they prove otherwise.
- Explain rather than blame. The result of a performance evaluation should produce a better—not bitter—individual or team performer.

## Mantra

All people have within themselves a combination of skills and interests that will allow them to achieve at a very high level. Most of those skills are subtle and therefore not obvious and not necessarily the ones they would choose. Success at the highest level is most often achieved by those who gain that insight. People cannot fully recognize which are their best skills without first being comfortable recognizing their own weaknesses. Remarkably, this is often a significant barrier for persons of high intellect.

## Life Lessons

- The effort it takes to achieve at the highest level is the best investment in time that a person can make. The additional satisfaction one achieves more than justifies the requirement of additional investment in time.
- As a business manager or leader, be intolerant of mediocre performance, not to be confused with mediocre talent. Marginally talented but dedicated people can be valuable employees. But mediocre performers are an organization's most expensive talent. Their presence keeps you from bringing in a good performer, and their work product usually needs shoring up by others in a distracting manner.
- Make career decisions based on enjoyment of the substance of the work rather than the level of compensation. People in careers they find meaningful find that the financial rewards usually follow.

## BUILDING YOUR PYRAMID

Kruszewski is the only CEO I know who uses the unique method of using a list of criteria to evaluate opportunities rather than using a formal plan. Life can be unpredictable. Sometimes the path you thought you were destined for takes a detour. But does that mean that you should stop following that path? No. Continue and see where it will take you. Being flexible as a leader and keeping your eyes open to all the possibilities will actually keep you on course. If you put blinders on, you will miss the view.

It takes courage, knowledge, and a teamwork mentality to make this level of the opportunity pyramid work. Kruszewski's impressive track record shows that if you have the right strategies in place and follow them, you can succeed in any business environment.

Here are my tips on how to do just that.

### If you are a business owner or manager:

Kruszewski exemplifies how important it is to lead with confidence. Staying the course can be difficult if those around you don't understand your goals. Kruszewski stuck to his core principles and educated his board about where he wanted to take the company.

Another trait you will need at this level of the pyramid is the ability to look at your faults or shortcomings. Everyone I interviewed for this book agreed that good leaders recognize areas in themselves that could use improvement. For Kruszewski, this area was his ability to listen; when he started at Stifel, he made it a point to strengthen his listening skills. By doing so, he was able to fix problems plaguing the organization. Listening is also necessary to effectively service customers. How can you fulfill the needs of your customers if you don't know what they want? Or, to consider it from a different perspective, do employees want to work for someone who doesn't take the time to hear what they are saying? Taking the time to listen is a huge morale booster. Nothing is worse than working for someone who doesn't listen to you because they think they already know everything.

Not only that, but by showing he is open to suggestions and change, Kruszewski is also setting an example for the organization's culture. How would you characterize your style? Is it open, nimble, and empowering like Kruszewski's? When you take the time to listen to your employees you help build up their confidence. Not only does this foster a positive environment, it can also help improve productivity. Listening and responding are ways to show you care. As Kruszewski puts it, "You have to invest a lot of authority with your key people. You motivate them, and they like it. This positive reinforcement builds the culture."

## If you are an employee:

You can help stay the course by listening to your superiors and executing to the best of your ability. If you are a service-based company and you work directly with customers, have an open dialogue with them. Don't be afraid to ask if there is anything you can do to serve them better. Questions like this can give you insight into how to improve your services. You might also gain repeat customers because they feel you value their opinions. This can open up areas of opportunity: if customers are complaining about a competitor and you find out why, you might be able to turn that into an opportunity to take away some market share from them.

Remember that the decisions you make and your execution will also impact your own career. If you are looking to move up, ask yourself: Will this help me achieve what I want in my next career move? If you are delegating and offering up new ideas, can that help you with a promotion?

## If you are an aspiring entrepreneur:

Listen to what's going on around you. Talk to customers and find out what they are looking for. This knowledge can help you prepare for opportunity. Be nimble—this is one of the assets that helped Kruszewski take advantage of opportunity. Recall Kruszewski's advice that good leaders are always evaluating, and they have a good business structure and expense model in place so when an opportunity presents itself, they are ready. Are you?

## FINAL THOUGHTS

The "staying the course" layer of the pyramid is where the previous layers begin to really cohere. Defining who you are and solidifying that definition with your mission statement help you boost your confidence and stay the course. Your knowledge in your field, coupled with the listening skills Kruszewski has spoken about, also reinforce this layer. With these different elements coming together, you are ready to embark on the next level: execution.

# 7    Execute—Pay Attention to the Details

## David Rubenstein

THE NEXT LAYER of our pyramid, execution, can launch you to the pinnacle of success if handled right. But one wrong move can set back or even sink your goal. Successfully achieving this step starts with paying attention to details. By carefully analyzing the details of a possible opportunity, you can then carry out your plan effectively. A leader who embodies such patience and attention to detail is David Rubenstein, cofounder and co-CEO of The Carlyle Group.

A lover of history and owner of one of the original copies of the Magna Carta, Rubenstein embraces our founding fathers' focus and clarity of execution. He has fostered a similar philosophy at Carlyle, one of the world's largest and most successful private equity firms. When you speak with Rubenstein, he is very direct and doesn't mince words—he never wavers or goes on a tangent. (Even his humor doesn't skip a beat. When he was guest cohosting CNBC's *Squawk Box* and the subject turned to the Olympics and Michael Phelps's 200-meter win, he dryly quipped, "I used to swim in the same pool as Michael Phelps and I'm still working on my 200 meters. It's been 12 years.")

Carlyle calls itself an "alternative asset manager," managing more than $150 billion from 32 offices around the world.[14] The company went public on May 3, 2012. Unlike hedge funds, which are all about short-term investments, the private equity industry focuses on long-term investments of four to six years. The time frame requires careful planning and attention to detail. To make the right decision on strategy, private equity firms need to evaluate various factors at both the macro and micro levels, analyzing the direction of the economy during that four-to-six-year period of time and potential industry changes.

Rubenstein explains, "The theory behind the longer time horizon was, by the time the six and seventh year arose and you sold your investment, you would have a compound and annualized rate of return of 25 to 30 percent. When you are orchestrating buyouts such as Carlyle does, you are looking at *improving* the operations of a company. You need to make sure you have a game plan that has been vetted as well as an execution plan so you can deploy your capital effectively. Time is an important factor when improving a company."

## STRATEGIES FOR SUCCESS

Carlyle's investments in Dunkin' Brands and Diversified Machine, Inc., are perfect examples of its strategy. Collectively, these investments have created more than 40,000 jobs and increased the value of those companies by 100 percent.[15] Although Carlyle's restructuring and reorganizing of companies has taken place on a grand scale, its detailed checklist to increase the value in its companies can apply to anyone:

- **Ensure the capital is available to invest.** This is important because in many cases, the companies Carlyle is investing in are capital short.
- **Bring in leadership.** Rubenstein explains that many times businesses get in trouble because the current leadership has been ineffective. Carlyle establishes a team to focus the business, sharpening the strategic vision and executing with precision.
- **Align management, employees, and owners.** This typically entails incentivizing employees to behave like owners, by having management invest its own money, or providing stakes to employees. Rubenstein says being an actual owner gives employees a new view of the business that results in increased productivity.

Managing capital well, focusing a business through strong leadership, and giving employees a stake in the business are things all business owners can do. This is all about building a culture that encourages leadership. You want to have a positive environment for your employees. The three strategies Rubenstein mentions are ways to create an encouraging atmosphere. Motivating change starts with the leader of the company; he or she is responsible for jumpstarting the organization's culture.

## CULTIVATING CULTURE

A company's culture is the essence of how managers and employees approach and execute plans, and this culture comes from the top. Management needs to put in place a clear set of objectives, and everyone in the organization has to believe in them to execute plans effectively.

Rubenstein's formula for creating a culture that fosters innovation and performance is the same in every Carlyle office around the globe. "We have a 'One Carlyle' culture, which means everyone is truly a member of one firm and they are incented to make sure they *work* as one firm, or they will be penalized if they don't," he explains. This framework provides the comfort of inclusion and the guidelines employees need to thrive.

When speaking with Carlyle employees, I got to see the One Carlyle culture at work. No matter who an employee was or what his or her position was within the organization, you could hear Rubenstein's (and fellow Carlyle cofounder Daniel D'Aniello's) long-term philosophy in the discussions. No matter which Carlyle office you are in around the world, the company's long-term philosophy is present in tangible items to remind employees that they are all in this together, from visual reminders on employees' desks to posters in the lunchrooms. One longtime employee told me this "reminds us [what] we stand for." I have been told it brings employees who visit the various offices around the world a nice source of comfort and camaraderie. Culture is a living, breathing creature. You have to nurture it and foster it over time. Rubenstein emphasizes the culture by awarding one employee in the world each year with a One Carlyle award. I have been told it is considered the highest honor that can be bestowed on an employee. And even outside the office, the culture influences discussion. My show *Squawk Box* airs live from the Baron Investment Conference each year. At the November 2013 conference, Glenn Youngkin, COO of Carlyle, discussed culture and business etiquette off camera. He said, "We have two rules—always return your calls and walk people to the elevator."

## HANDLING THE PRESSURE FOR RESULTS

Executing effectively is especially crucial in times of crisis, when there is panic in the markets. During the 2008 financial crisis, there were runs on hedge funds because investors wanted their money back and pulled it out of the markets. For the private equity industry, investors who understood the long-term time horizon also started clamoring to see returns a lot faster. In response, some in the private equity industry drastically changed their time horizons: "The four- to six-year investment got compressed to three to five years, and then down to two to three years," says Rubenstein. "Sometimes, the sale was as quick as a pre-IPO investment, so you could get your money back very quickly."

But while many in the industry felt the pressure to perform financially, Rubenstein didn't waver from his investment strategy. This is key at this level of the opportunity pyramid. Rubenstein explains, "I don't think it is always good to have a short-term investment horizon. If you are able to have a long-term horizon, you will probably do well because you are going to counter the general population."

When leaders go against the grain of the competition, they need to effectively communicate their message to investors. Rubenstein's message is very similar to that of one of the world's most successful investors. As he puts it, "Warren Buffett says he has a time horizon of forever, and he has obviously done very well. If you are willing to hold onto something for four, five, six years, or even longer, you can probably make a company very, very valuable. It's the pressure to resolve something in one year, two years, that often gets you in trouble." Carlyle is all about creating value, and the shorter time frame would put a squeeze on how much value it could add to a company. This value ultimately determines what kind of return Carlyle gets when it sells a company or takes it public. Rubenstein focuses on striking a compromise between investors' expectations and his long-term strategy.

Rubenstein refused to follow the private-equity pack with its drastic return horizons. As Ron Baron, a quintessential buy-and-hold investor, once told me, "In order to build something you need a different perspective." Standing by your principles can be hard, but in the end, if you chase instead of lead, you will always be a follower. It is also important to know when you need to change course. Leaders need to be committed to their overall goals but flexible enough to know that sometimes plans should change. Rubenstein's slightly shortened investment timeline is a good example.

## NO INSTANT GRATIFICATION

Attaining the pinnacle of success takes time. There is no easy path to achieving your goal. All of my contacts, including the billionaires, work tirelessly. Their work ethic and focus are immeasurable. Rubenstein says one of the biggest challenges facing business leaders today is our culture of instant gratification, which is the driver behind the abbreviated investment timeline: "The lack of attention is a byproduct of this. We want results now. We want information now. We want news now. As a society, waiting for something and deferring gratification is something we just aren't good at." This type of thinking can impact execution because the focus is on the moment, not the whole picture. Many of my contacts have expressed the idea that you can't manage a business by leading just for the here and now. You have to manage based on what you believe the company *will* be. Don't make it up as you go along or react moment to moment. Developing a plan takes time and you need to focus by disregarding pressures from the outside.

Let me share how I have applied this lesson to my own career. As a television journalist, it is my responsibility to make sure that when I produce or report on a story, I show the whole picture. In order to do that, I need to make sure all of my details are accurate—if they don't add up, we don't report the story. For example, I once received a call from a congressman's office telling me the representative was going to accuse a regulator of wrongdoing. Of course, one of my competitors was also working that story, so there was pressure to break the news. But the quest to be first can sometimes lead to sloppiness. How many times have you seen networks get their facts wrong because they wanted to be the first to break a story? Too many, as far as I'm concerned. The blunder is a credibility killer.

Back to my story. Immediately, once I got the details from the representative's office, I started fact-checking to see if the story was true. After several hours on the phone trying to verify the accusation, I found out that the representative's source—the entire basis of his accusation—was not credible. We decided to abandon the story.

Clearly, dedicating time and attention to vetting and research is imperative in this step of the opportunity pyramid. You can't execute if you don't have your facts right and your strategy in place. But in our technology-driven world, where people focus on instantaneous information and responses, Rubenstein often ponders how the values of yesterday and today collide. "People tend to not have the long-term horizons they used to have," he says. "How many children do you think can sit down today and read *War and Peace* without feeling they will have to be interrupted a thousand times before they finish it? I often wonder: if Thomas Jefferson were alive today, could he have spent four consecutive days writing the Declaration of Independence without having to worry about emails, Google Alerts coming in, and so forth? The attention span that people have today is limited."

## COMPETITION GOES RIGHT, HE GOES LEFT

Differentiating oneself from the competition is crucial at this level of the pyramid. Rubenstein's own pioneering moment has proven to be one of his most lucrative, all because of details he saw before his competition even noticed. That moment was blazing an investment trail in China.

Recognizing the strength of a trend in China's food market, Carlyle seized the moment by doing research, executing, and never looking back. Carlyle made several key investments in food, all of which were plays on the rise of the middle class. One of them was a strategic minority stake in an infant formula company, because "milk becomes more important as populations grow." Rubenstein explains that they also "invested in a fisheries company that's harvesting fish in a sustainable way and feeding the population of China. And our other investment is in a grain production company that grows grain that is used in China. China is and will continue to be one of the most attractive emerged markets to invest in over the next five to ten years." Under Rubenstein's leadership, Carlyle has become the largest private-equity investor in China and China has become one of Carlyle's largest sources of profits to date.

Rubenstein explains that the largest emerging markets—Brazil, China, India, Korea, Taiwan, Mexico, Saudi Arabia, Turkey—are growing 5 to 10 percent a year. "They have large population bases, pretty stable economies, and pretty good currencies relative to the United States," he says. "We've been focusing on the larger emerging markets, which I like to call the 'emerged markets.' They're the ones I think present the greatest opportunities for the foreseeable future for private equity investors."

"Future" is the key word here. Rubenstein is always looking ahead. He does not use the word "now" in any of his investing discussions. Based on the success of this investing strategy, Rubenstein says he expects Carlyle to make similar kinds of investments in other parts of the world where populations are very large. This speaks to Carlyle's culture of consistency.

## THE DEVIL'S IN THE DETAILS

Rubenstein shared the questions his teams ask when they evaluate a possible investment. These questions help break down the details of each opportunity before execution:

- Is this a company you would be proud to own because it does something useful and makes a product or service that people should have, or need to have?
- Does the company have a management team that can make the company more valuable than it has been? If not, can a management team be developed that will achieve this?
- Can the management team and the firm (Carlyle) make enough of a change so that the rate of return for the firm's investors would be worth the effort Carlyle puts into it?

"It's not because of our charm that we've raised so much money," Rubenstein says. "It's because of the rates of return we have generated. Our top four funds have been very good. In the end, we are always working for our investors with our mission of effectuating a 20 to 25 percent rate of return on something after four to six years."

## PROFITING OFF OF POLITICAL UNCERTAINTY

The headwinds facing the business community have substantially increased over the past few years. The root of this uncertainty has been government, regardless of where you stand politically. One of the biggest concerns I have heard from business leaders around the world involves the inaction of politicians. From the proverbial kicking of the can over the deficit debate to the sovereign debt crisis, business owners face a tremendous amount of political uncertainty whose outcome could hugely impact their companies.

This uncertainty leaves many business owners frozen with inaction. But despite this, leaders can learn a lot from people like Rubenstein about the need to rise and continue to plot their course amid political changes. You can't grow standing still. Formerly the deputy domestic policy advisor to President Jimmy Carter, Rubenstein is well-versed in politics. He says that "great fortunes have been made, and will always be made, depending on what a government does." He continues, "If you take a look at the greatest investments ever made, many of those investments have taken advantage of either a legislative change or regulatory change. If someone can figure out what those changes will be in advance, they'll probably do reasonably well if they pursue the right niches."

You don't need White House experience to do what Rubenstein has done. You just need to look out for trends, use your prior experiences to your advantage, and apply old-fashioned common sense. For example, Rubenstein looked at patterns in GDP when he decided to invest in health care: "When I worked in the White House as a young man, health care was 3 percent of GDP. Now it's about 18 percent and heading up as my generation of baby boomers begins to retire." And look for the "dogs" of an industry. Just because a sector gets hit doesn't mean all the companies in that sector are bad investments. Review the details to see which companies have growth potential. For example, Rubenstein says the financial services sector was unbelievably depressed as a result of the Great Recession, which created opportunities for those who wanted to take the time to research: "Asset management companies, banking companies, insurance companies—all of them have been beaten down a bit, so those are areas that are pretty attractive."

## RISK AND EXECUTION

The last step to take before executing a plan is addressing downside risk. You can't always anticipate what all the risks will be, but Rubenstein says you need to at least acknowledge them. "We always have a fear that something will go wrong," he acknowledges. "When private equity people do deals, they typically take six to nine months to do the due diligence. What they are spending most of their time on is what can go wrong"—in other words, calculating risk.

After analyzing downside risk, Carlyle's team creates a list of specific actions to address downside protection. Rubenstein says, "You don't get 25 to 30 percent rates of return without taking risk. To help moderate these possible risks, Carlyle does a lot of due diligence." Fear of a misstep is not part of the equation. "If you are afraid of making a mistake and losing money, then you can't be in the deals world," according to Rubenstein. "Private equity is not for the faint of heart. If you are an investor who never wants to lose money or take risks, you should probably buy treasury bills or something like that."

Of course, even if you're not in private equity, risk is a natural part of running any business. As a leader, you have to have the stomach for it. In Carlyle's two-plus decades, Rubenstein says, they have probably lost 5 to 6 percent of their capital, but they've averaged gross 30 percent gains overall, which more than compensates for the risks they have taken.

Getting a long-term return like this, of course, takes patience. In a world where news is becoming increasingly arcane and smartphones rule the information highway, waiting for something can be a challenge. The reason for Rubenstein's success, though, is that all the layers of Carlyle's pyramid are solidly in place. Carlyle's leaders know who they are, they strengthen their knowledge on a daily basis with their analysis and research, and their passion drives their commitment to staying the course. Using the steps Rubenstein has employed can offer you the focus and consistency you need to rise to the next level of the opportunity pyramid.

A Page from My Notebook: **David Rubenstein**

### Words to Live By

- Hard work and perseverance—which means long hours—will generally enable me to achieve my desired goals, and may help to overcome other personal deficiencies or weaknesses.
- Skills of communicating well, through written or spoken means, are rarer than they should be; therefore, spending time on trying to communicate well will usually help with the achievement of desired goals.
- Having a fair degree of humility, as well as sharing credit and rewards, will help enormously in achieving professional and personal objectives.

- I try to remember where I came from—a family of modest means and educational attainment—to make certain I stay grounded; and I try to understand where others come from to better understand their likely motivations, ambitions, and needs.
- If good fortune should strike, it is important to give back much of that good fortune to help others in one's community or society; to help them reach their own objectives and to achieve some measure of good fortune as well.
- I try to remember that hard work and good fortune aside, luck is an important part of life, and those who have had good luck are not necessarily better people than those who have had bad luck.

## Mantra

Work hard; keep your ego in check; give back; and try to make the world a better place than you found it.

## Life Lessons

- Courtesies to other people will always be remembered and appreciated.
- A person's greatest asset is his or her reputation.
- Hard work and perseverance are generally rewarded, but a little luck doesn't hurt.
- Conventional wisdom is almost always wrong.
- A focus on long-term goals will produce far greater benefits than a focus on short-term goals.
- Little can be accomplished by one person; a team is needed for real success and accomplishments.
- Money is ephemeral; do not let chasing it distort higher goals and priorities.

## BUILDING YOUR PYRAMID

Rubenstein and his team may not be able to control the volatile emotions of investors and the swings of the markets, but that doesn't mean they are powerless, either. Carlyle has been able to rise above the competition by keeping its focus and control by sticking with its culture and not deviating from its core investing principles.

Here are my tips on applying Rubenstein's business philosophy:

### If you are a business owner or manager:

One of the biggest challenges facing executives, managers, and small business owners is blocking out the noise of the here and now and focusing on the details of the future. Between texting, emails, tweets, Facebook statuses, and even online shopping, the craving for quick results has never been stronger. The term "CrackBerry" was coined for a reason.

In order to effectively circumvent distractions, Rubenstein stresses the need to pay attention to details on both the macro and micro levels and the advantage of time when investing in a company. Adding time is an important factor when "improving a company" (Rubenstein's words)—the more time you have, the better. Rubenstein shows you how this gift of time has enabled his team to pace itself in planning, researching, and executing.

Since Carlyle is a private equity company, its timetable is four to six years. What kind of time frame do you have? Even with competitors drastically cutting their time frames to chase customer's expectations, Rubenstein didn't cave under time pressures. He responded carefully— by slightly modifying Carlyle's time frame to acknowledge the present environment, without hampering its investing plan. This is proof that you can react nimbly while remaining committed to a plan. Life is a compromise, and so is business.

Having a larger time frame enables the members of Carlyle to get a broader picture of the business landscape. Trying to satisfy both your short-term and long-term needs is definitely a balancing act. Rubenstein shows you that if you stick to your research and not let the distractions of the here and now take you off course you should be able to execute your plan.

Another lesson from Rubenstein's story is to carefully research risks before taking them. The knowledge Rubenstein and his employees gain from their months of research gives them the confidence they need to make calculated decisions. Just like Kruszewski emphasized in his discussion with me, they anticipate what the possible risks could be and then they figure out how they'd handle them. "We always have a fear that something will go wrong," he says, but acknowledging that fear is part of their strategy.

Finally, pay attention to people and culture in order to execute your plans effectively. Through Rubenstein's One Carlyle culture, the company has been able to foster innovation and performance in all of their offices around the world. Recall Rubenstein's strategy: "[Our employees] are incented to make sure they work as one firm, or they will be penalized if they don't." How do you incentivize your workers? Besides monetary rewards, Rubenstein also spoke about the importance of communicating with workers and customers. People want to know what will happen next. Of course you can't predict the future, but telling your workers and customers about your plans and intentions helps manage expectations.

## If you are an employee:

When you are a part of the team you play an important role in the company's execution of its plans, so you need to pay attention to the details. No matter if you're working as a cashier, in an accounting office, or a Fortune 500 company, your productivity depends on your attention to details. This means taking time to focus on your work and not rushing through anything.

Communication is also pivotal on your part. Just as your manager needs to communicate clearly with you from the top down, you need to communicate "up" to your manager as well. How can the organization execute effectively if everyone isn't on the same page?

## If you are an aspiring entrepreneur:

This level of the pyramid can be quite challenging, because not only are you trying to build a business, you are also working day to day. Organization is a must. You don't want to rush through things to jumpstart your new chapter in life. You need to self-edit your career and the steps you will take in order to make your entrepreneurial dreams come true, just as I will edit this book on its way to publication. Remember to set a timetable and do your due diligence in analyzing possible outcomes.

If you take this journey slowly and steadily, you may find your path changes slightly along the way. That's OK. As you will see in the next chapter, being wedded to an idea can hold you back. Your dreams can morph into something even better. So see where they take you.

---

## FINAL THOUGHTS

Leveraging the minutes and hours is crucial in building this level of the pyramid. Remember that slow and steady wins the race. You are building layers up slowly, and they take time to set. If you move on to build the next level and the glue isn't ready, the pyramid can collapse. If you take your time and set out how you will execute your plan, all the hard work in the previous layers of the pyramid will fall into place. You need a fortified pyramid to take you to the last level, or apex, of the pyramid: world domination.

# 8

# Think Ahead—
# World Domination

## Lisa Stone, Elisa Camahort Page,
## and Jory Des Jardins

W|E HAVE FINALLY reached the top of the opportunity pyramid, and it's all about domination. Yes, that's a bold goal—but who doesn't want to be the best? To get there, though, we often need a little kick. We need to leave our comfort zones. Lisa Stone, Elisa Camahort Page, and Jory Des Jardins, the three founders of the web community BlogHer, did just that. These three women were very candid when they told me why they all left safe, stable careers for the unknown. They did it because they shared a common goal: they wanted to be happy.

Each of these women had a separate wake-up call and realized her career was not fulfilling. What I find fascinating about them is that they created an empire out of nothing. When they started, there was no blogging "community." The Internet was a vast ocean where bloggers drifted. Stone, Camahort Page, and Des Jardins created a home for millions of women bloggers to voice their opinions and thoughts. Today, BlogHer has expanded to include an ad network, an annual conference, and a blogging network.

I've said it before and I'll say it again: I am very lucky to be working in an industry I love. Sure, I have stress and deal with unpleasant personalities at times, but I can honestly say I love what I do. Life is too short to do something you don't like, and I could not imagine doing anything else. Work is such a large part of your life—why not do something you enjoy?

The three founders of BlogHer feel the same way. Their company was established in 2005 and has grown into a social media powerhouse for women. Reaching more than 45 million unique visitors monthly, it is one of the top 100 web properties in the United States, and has the highest concentration of women of those 100 properties. BlogHer acts as a publisher for 15,000 influencers (bloggers), who reach 92 million people across blogs and social tools, including 55 million blog readers. BlogHer generates revenue by conducting advertising and marketing campaigns and by hosting a series of live events.[16]

Blogging has certainly transformed from its early days. In contrast to the blogs of the nineties that featured "escribitionists" who wrote online diaries and technology writers who dissected product releases, today's blogs are forums for shaping news. Bloggers have voiced passionate points of view on the Iraq War and even had a hand in US Senate Majority Leader Trent Lott stepping down from Congress. Today, blogs are a way for those with an insatiable appetite for news to both report it and receive it. Even politicians tweet, blog, and Facebook their thoughts to the masses. Bill Daley, former chief of staff for President Obama, told me he was amazed how much social media has played a role in the 2013 debt ceiling debate.

Stone, Camahort Page, and Des Jardins were reflective, energetic, and enthusiastic when I spoke with them. The synergies among their answers to my questions help explain why this company has blazed a path of success that many executives dream of but few have achieved. Passion, undying spirit, and drive for "world domination," as Camahort Page puts it, are just some of the ingredients in their organization's recipe for success. As you read their story, you can see the building blocks of success that went into crafting the apex of their opportunity pyramid.

## THE COURAGE TO LEAVE

The paths the three founders have taken are different, but they all demonstrate the importance of having the courage of pack up your life and try something new. For Stone, the year of change was 1997. She was a chief strategist for CNN, had a one-year-old, and was getting divorced.

Realizing she was going to have to provide for her baby and could no longer travel as part of her job, she started looking for the next chapter in her career. "At CNN, I spent my time split between San Francisco and Atlanta," she says. "Living in the Bay Area, I was very familiar with Silicon Valley and I was very excited there was an opportunity for WebTV. At the time the leading opinion about women online was that women really didn't go online—but I realized my entire life was online. I was galvanized about going online, and I was able to use my career and my background from CNN. After [several] months of WebTV where I parlayed my TV experience into online experience, I joined Women.com as a senior and executive producer and ultimately became the editor in chief. Women.com became the number-one site for women and was acquired by iVillage in 2001."

Camahort Page, on the other hand, started out in Silicon Valley. She worked in product-line management for a company that provided the hardware for cable operators to deliver Internet. Ironically, she was not a huge Internet user back then. She says, "I emailed and used the Internet only for work. During the dot-com boom and bust, I worked at a good company, but I was burned out."

She didn't fully know it at the time, but her entrepreneurial spirit was burning. She says, "I also kind of realized when you work for other people there's a point when your authority ends, and you have to act based on the decisions you may not agree with because they are coming from people who are over your head." Her moment came when the company began laying off workers. She wasn't one of them. "That weekend I was depressed that I was not on the list and I thought, well that's a bad sign; that's not good," she says. "Even in a bust one should not have those thoughts. So on Monday, I went to the person who was overseeing the layoffs and I asked them if it was not too late to be put on the list. Turns out they did not want me to leave. I stayed for six more weeks and then I consulted with them for an additional four months. Some people thought I was crazy to walk away from a good job during a bad time for the industry, but I was very thrifty and had saved two years' salary, plus I was consulting."

Camahort Page started blogging during her time as a consultant, after she received a free piece of software from her mac.com membership. "I started playing with it and I was writing my opinions on politics and movie, theatre, and book reviews. I discovered one of the number-one motivators of bloggers is simply self-expression, and I loved it."

That passion fueled her career, and it didn't take too long for her new blog to offer up a positive turning point. It came when she wrote a review for a local Greek restaurant: "Most Greek delis in Silicon Valley are not that good, but this one in particular was very good," she says. "So I emailed people at my old company, sending them the link to my blog review on the restaurant. A couple of weeks later there are 10 people from my old company at this restaurant. So I asked them, 'Hey, why are you here?' And they told me, 'We read your review on your blog and it became a lunch place for the company.' I had what I like to call my peanut-butter-and-chocolate moment about blogging and marketing going well together, and about using blogging as a way of communications. I had no intention of starting my own business, but then I realized I wasn't working that hard or motivated to go back to my old way of life. So I decided to start doing marketing consulting, focusing on the online community and blogs. It was really out of the blue for me."

For Des Jardins, the story begins in New York City. She never considered herself an "astute businessperson" and she knew corporate life wasn't for her. Early in her career, she worked in book publishing, but a constrained progression up the food chain didn't appeal to her at all. She says, "I have this joke about book publishing—you get in and you're an editorial assistant and then the next year your an assistant editor and the next year you're an associate editor and the next year you just have to hold on ... all you need to do is not get fired and then you get your card punched every year. I thought, man, this really sucks. I thought it would work for me, but it didn't, so I left a number of times. I left the print world when I was 25 and went to work on my own things, and I found out that while it was terrifying, it was exhilarating. There was just something there that felt really good."

Sometimes in order to know you are doing the right thing, you need to leave it behind for a while. Des Jardins went back to corporate life three times before she made a clean break. She couldn't shake that nagging feeling that her future was out of her hands. But around 2004, when she first started blogging, she had a feeling she never felt before: empowerment. Her first blog was actually about fully embracing your entrepreneurial spirit: "My readers would send me these apologetic notes saying they're sorry they took a job, and I think my response was, 'Forgive yourself. That's fine.' We all have to do what's best for us, but I would also tell them they have not reached their 'point' yet. I had just reached my point. It was so powerful doing my own thing that it got to the point that the risk of not doing it outweighed the risk of doing it."

Des Jardins took the plunge with no idea how she would make money. She told me about the advice she gave others on how to start a business from her blog: "I always said to try to do little projects on the side. Yes, it takes a lot of energy to do something early and try to get out there. But it's not that entrepreneurial to say you are going to leave, and *then* start your business. I've told [people], 'You're not ready, because if you were ready, you would already be making calls, sneaking out at lunch, and doing what you need to do in order to start your business.'"

She also emphasizes the need to stay focused on the endgame— on the apex of your pyramid. "Eventually you make the leap," she says. "It's always the end goal. Not, 'I'm going to take this small step, see if it works, and then I'm going to be an entrepreneur.' You always have that leap as your end goal. It may take longer than you think, and you may stay in a corporation for a long time or do something other than your new business, but it's always your end goal to leave and do your business full time."

The common thread for these three women was their courage to face the future. They didn't like the paths they were on, so they decided to look within and tap their strengths to start their own businesses. If you are passionate about something, chances are you will excel at it, but you have to give 110 percent, as the cliché says. In order to reach your apex of success, you need to have this type of passion and determination. Many people think it's crazy that I'm a mom to three busy children and also work full time at a television network and write, but you know what? I love it. I find the time because I enjoy what I do (and yes, I do sleep).

## BIRDS OF A FEATHER

As you've seen throughout this book, creating a culture that encourages growth starts with the leaders. This is true of any leader, not just CEOs of large conglomerates. Des Jardins, Stone, and Camahort Page, like Steve Case, are people who defined their own opportunities by creating a space on the Internet that didn't exist until they came along.

The story of how they built BlogHer started with a simple "hello." Just a week or so after Des Jardins quit her job, she was attending a blogging conference. "What's funny about a blogging conference," she chuckled as she spoke to me, "is no one is looking at you. Everyone is on the computer staring straight ahead, typing. But there was one person looking up, and it was Elisa. We got to talking, and she told me she met a gal name Lisa Stone, and they both really loved blogging and they wanted to create an event for women bloggers. I immediately thought that was really cool."

This idea progressed in talks for several months, and Des Jardins says the idea just kept sucking her in. She went to go find a venue where they could host an event to attract other bloggers like themselves. The events they'd attended in the past felt like they were lacking something. They wanted to create an event experience that would leave themselves and other female bloggers energized and coming back for more. That was when the light bulb went on. "I realized we were on to something. I had no idea if this was going to be a money-maker, or that we would be attracting people. It was just a thing that I wanted to go to. The idea was very organic. This came from within [rather than being] something that I 'should' be doing. Sure, if I wanted to be a writer maybe I 'should' be working at a publishing house. But this idea was much more. I wanted to be a part of it."

The three women became joined at the hip as they made plans, driven to create an event they themselves would want to participate in. According to Des Jardins, "There was a point, maybe three months [after] we started this, that someone wanted to interview us because they heard about the blogging conference. The three of us were like, 'Why do you want to interview us?' After the interview she asked, 'What shall I call you?' and Lisa said, 'Well, we're cofounders.' And that's when I realized we created something."

## LEADING BY LISTENING

All three founders will tell you that at BlogHer's foundation lies their ability to listen. "You have to learn by listening," says Stone. "When we started BlogHer, people were asking us, 'Where were the women blogging?' We knew they were everywhere, but the only way you could possibly get the word out is not by talking about it but by showing it." Listening is also important because it helps you measure your ideas—a good idea is one that grows and attracts others.

Using what they learned from other blogging experiences, the three founders agreed the event should be a living, breathing, evolving idea. According to Des Jardins, "Rather than telling bloggers what the sessions were going to be and how the experience would be, it was this constant curation. What we did was simply build a business based on what we would have wanted as bloggers ourselves."

Stone added that this counterintuitive approach was their key to success: "We said, 'OK, online community, what do you want? What is your motivation? What do you want to accomplish with your blog? With your family and with your life?' And based on that, we developed different opportunities for them to communicate, which also became a great business model."

The success of BlogHer, which was created before both Facebook and Twitter, caught the eyes of advertisers. Around that time, studies substantiated the influence of women bloggers, and their tendency to talk about products started resonating with marketers. "Women are not only the majority of voters, but we are also the majority of Internet users," explains Stone. "And women are the majority of users who use social media on a weekly basis. According to our own research in conjunction with Nielsen, 55.6 million women are in the blogosphere every month writing, reading, and commenting. These women are also the group that controls 83 percent of household discretionary spending. So, when you look at the users we are reaching, they are highly educated, and very focused on voting [and] improving the world around them."

All good business owners need to know their target audience in order to grow their company. The more you know about your customers, the better your ability to serve. The BlogHer founders did their research. They know the majority of women BlogHer reaches are married and have children under 18 at home. According to Stone, the typical female blogger "is using her blogs to talk about everything—from what products she buys, to who she is going to vote for. This leadership attracts companies, because it gives them better insight into targeting their consumer. After all, 87 percent of our users say they have purchased a product based on a recommendation of a blogger. Companies have seized on this, recognizing the opportunity of a blogger's word. Trust is what it's all about. If you're a brand and you are not participating in a space to talk about yourself or your brand, you will not reach them. You need to be out there in order to be heard."

When asked what inning their industry would be in if it were a ballgame, Camahort Page says she thinks the blogosphere is in its third or fourth inning: "You know you have some momentum. The crowd is getting into it, and hopefully it is turning into a pitching battle or a hitting game, but there are some exciting things happening. I still see it as early in the game for blogging and social tools, even though reading blogs has become mainstream for the average American. Our latest study shows more than three quarters of Americans who go online use some form of social media every week, but advertiser dollars haven't followed yet, and we're all still trying to figure out the best business models for mobile and online video. So, the growth so far is really just the tip of the iceberg." She continues, "There are still a lot of industries trying to figure out how to tap into this community. There is a ton of opportunity. Women bloggers are getting more business savvy to meet that opportunity."

"It was a perfect storm of data, and BlogHer had already created an opportunity around it," explains Des Jardins. "I saw it as this revolution of women who realized they could write and build a platform, and then brands became involved. Companies would invite us to speak about bloggers, and that would lead to business. We were onto something that companies cared about. But it also put the onus of responsibility on us, because these companies were looking to us for best blogging practices. There were no rules, and there was a lot of criticism of the blogosphere because of that, so someone needed to set the tone for engagement. That was us. It was a role we hadn't anticipated. We needed to lead in order to carve the path for the future. So in 2006 we built an editorial standard."

In order to add credibility to the site, the three saw the need to separate advertising and editorial content. "We put quality first. We requested of women in our network to credit their links and separate church and state—editorial on one side, advertising on the other. This made it possible for people to trust them," explains Stone.

This also created a way for the company to diversify their business model: "We would split our advertising with you 50–50 because you are going to be paid for your writing," Des Jardins says. Camahort Page adds, "Social media is also a way of communicating. People are sending messages via Facebook instead of email. Now do I think that will replace email? No, but there is a need to communicate and commune with people, to develop friendships. It's very different than traditional media, where you watch and don't participate. Personal expression and participation are two things people gravitate to when it comes to blogging. That's why social media has a strong future and will thrive, because it serves the basic need of communicating."

## LEARNING HOW TO GROW

Like other successful business owners before them, the founders of BlogHer soon came to the realization that they would have to grow in order to meet demand. Growth was—and still is—a scary and thrilling process. When they realized it was impossible for the three of them to curate the entire process, they used a hub-and-spoke system to grow their company and allow their culture to thrive. "We noticed from our conference there was a group of women who were loyal and wanted to help," explains Des Jardins. "They were our first farm team. Many of them are now working at BlogHer full time and we have grown that out."

By hiring people who embrace their outlook on blogging, they have continued to grow their company. One of the niche areas back in 2005 was "mommy blogging," which has since transformed into one of the biggest blogging segments with over four million mommy bloggers generating multibillions of dollars as companies place ads on their sites. One of the pioneers in this space was Jenny Lauck, now the organization's VP of publishing. Lauck spoke on the first-ever mommy blogging panel at the first BlogHer conference. "She stayed in touch with us as we began to grow; she had a very community-minded way about her. When she spoke, people listened," says Des Jardins. "So when we grew the company she became a community manager and a 'blogger whisperer.' And now she has trained an entire team of bloggers to do the same. She is the perfect example of one of the 'spokes' out in the community."

Des Jardins stresses that you cannot teach the passion that permeates their organization: "What's more problematic for us is hiring someone from outside the organization and hoping they get it. Culture is so hugely important to BlogHer. The moment we get cocky, that's the day we will drop the ball. The one thing technology has enabled is [that] the minute you screw up, everyone knows. So when you talk about culture, everyone has to live it. You'll fail if you don't. I do think there are tactical elements to creating a positive culture. When we bring in someone new to the management team, they meet the founders. If I'm not personally hiring that position, I just talk to them for a while. We have been addressing this, because as we get bigger and bigger it will be very hard for someone to sit down and have lunch with Elisa, Lisa, and myself. However, from the beginning we've laid out what we are about."

When asked what advice she would give to aspiring bloggers who want to get their message out, Stone said, "Ask yourself, 'How do I build a business by providing a service that no one else has provided?' In order to be acknowledged by a community, you have to participate in that community. In today's information economy, it's essential to read, as well as [to] be read. In fact, read first—offer comments first, offer your opinions and your attention to someone else—in order to receive theirs in return. You have to have credibility in order to get recommended. Buzz comes from people who recommend you based on the quality of your participation."

With social media still evolving, these online trailblazers are constantly looking at the landscape and asking how to evolve their company to stay ahead. Des Jardins stresses: "We now integrate Twitter, Facebook, and new technologies into our programs. We always ask ourselves, 'What are we missing?' And we will continue to ask that question. It is a question anyone who has had success in an area should be asking themselves—'Will I remain relevant?' We have never rested on our laurels. It is a constant tapping process. And while we may have become more comfortable in our business and how we run things, we are always refining our own processes, seeing what's out there. That's why I always say you can't get too wedded to what something will look like. You just have to go with change while remaining true to your mission. Give up on what it looks like, and let it grow."

## WORLD DOMINATION

In addition to being flexible to change, one of the most important skills of a successful businessperson is the ability to acknowledge the reality of a situation and realize you do not always have all the answers. According to Stone, "The growth trajectory of a startup is very difficult to plot out." In order to grow, you need capital. Camahort Page continued: "We bootstrapped it for a really long time. I went through my entire two years of savings, opened a home equity line of credit, and racked up credit card debt. We were paying a lot of people and not always paying ourselves. We saw this growth and knew there would be more growth. It was obvious we needed to make a living, and [that] we could grow this company but we needed the manpower and infrastructure to support it. We also had demand from companies who wanted to reach tens of millions of bloggers. With our size at the time, we knew we had to grow in order to meet that demand."

At first the trio was hesitant to take that step because they didn't want an outside investor to come in and change the product. But Des Jardins says they realized they needed to get over that fear to make this very important decision. "If someone was going to achieve world domination in this space, it was going to be us and not someone else. So we decided to go and get outside funding so we could take BlogHer to the next level," she says.

The injection of inorganic cash gave them the ability to expand their business. "It is pretty consuming when you're going through this. Making the decision about taking funding puts you at a crossroads, and I would totally recommend putting it off for as long as you can," Des Jardins says. "By the time we went to seek funding we had revenue. We had been growing a business for two years. When we made projections, they were based on real-world experience that we'd had with the network. So it put us in a very different position than if it was just an idea and we were in the beginning phases. We could say how we would spend that money and how it would help the business model. We had specifics." This is, crucially, how the previous layers of the pyramid come together to support the peak—world domination. The BlogHer founders had a wide base of knowledge and a strategy in place, so they were able to analyze this opportunity and let it launch them into success.

The founders stress that when they did seek funding, they never went to anyone with a five-year business plan. "We didn't think that was realistic," says Des Jardins, reflecting a mindset similar to that of Ron Kruszewski. "We don't think many five-year business plans are worth much. They don't reflect reality. We really try to keep focus on our current goals and work beyond the next year or two. There are a lot of macro issues that you have to be responsive to. With the economy imploding in 2008, if you had a five-year plan it would have been worth nothing. It changed how everyone was running a business. You had to be able to react and be flexible. I think the culture of Silicon Valley values agility and responsiveness. Either you have it and you can succeed, or you don't."

When taking their company to the level they describe as "world domination," Stone, Camahort Page, and Des Jardins asked themselves some key questions. You can ask yourself these same questions at this stage of the pyramid:

· How large do you envision your company being?
· Are you happy with what you are doing? Are you passionate about it?
· Are you satisfied doing it incrementally (in phases or stages)?
· Do you want a "lifestyle business," or is your goal "world domination"?

Explaining this last question, Camahort Page says, "In a 'lifestyle business,' you do make a reasonable living and have a nice business. You are your own boss and it's awesome. You may not have to work 24/7, but you may not be driving towards a much bigger opportunity. So I think it's worthwhile to ask yourself, How much will you work?" This part of the conversation really resonated with me the most; it really is the fundamental question in this layer of the opportunity pyramid. How much would it kill you to see someone else get really successful with your original idea, or what you think you're good at? Are you really willing to give up "world domination" in the area you're passionate about?

Only you know the answer, and it lies within your heart and soul.

## BUILDING YOUR PYRAMID

The story of BlogHer is a wonderful example of creation and of the ability to recognize the crossroads at which many businesses, both large and small, find themselves. When do you need to take it to the next level in order to achieve your own definition of "world domination"? The BlogHer founders define world domination differently from me, and you will define it differently from both of us. The bottom line is that you want to be the best in your niche or field. You can be a trailblazer—it doesn't matter if you are an employee, business owner, or aspiring entrepreneur. You just need to harness the fire in your belly, sow the seeds of your idea, and take action. The three founders of BlogHer were not afraid to fail. They wanted to be happy and fulfilled. What about you?

## A Page from Our Notebook: **Lisa Stone, Elisa Camahort Page, and Jory Des Jardins**

### Rules to Live By

**Stone:** Confidence is the heartbeat of beauty. The trick? To get there we have to fail and change. The courage to fail is irresistible to me.

### Mantra

**Camahort Page:** The corollary to living your values is: Do the best that you can, until you can do better. None of us is perfect. But we should never do nothing because we can't do everything.

### Life Lessons

**Des Jardins:** What are you always telling yourself you'll do "someday"? Consider doing it now. Note I didn't say to do it, but to consider doing it. Asking yourself to consider it takes the pressure off acting right away—but the seeds are subconsciously planted.

## If you are a business owner or manager:

Achieving world domination is very subjective, of course—you may define it differently than the BlogHer founders. Do you want a lifestyle business where you live comfortably or do you want to be the leader in your space?

The BlogHer founders described an injection of capital being what they needed to reach the apex of their pyramid, but just as important as capital is the commitment you are willing to put in. Commitment cements this level of the pyramid. Remember that you set the example for your team. You have been the creator of the culture and the mission statement; the source of passion, focus, and determination. Why would you want to cut corners when you have painstakingly kept an eye on the details, enriching your staff with knowledge and confidence? At this layer of the pyramid, all of the strategies you have mastered on this journey come together. You can't be afraid to try for world domination. As Des Jardins says, "The risk of not doing it outweighed the risk of doing it."

One of the biggest lessons to learn from these women is not to become complacent. Remember the two questions they constantly ask themselves:

- What are we missing?
- Will we remain relevant?

As you ask yourself these questions, remember not to stay married to what you think your business "should" look like. By being flexible and nimble your organization can grow to heights than you have never imagined. Most importantly remember to continue with your building blocks. If you veer off your mission statement, you could end up like Ford before Alan Mulally got there—adrift in the industry. You can never forget the lessons you have learned. When you are at the peak of performance, your attention to detail is imperative.

## If you are an employee:

When you work within an organization, your version of world domination might be a promotion that would lead in turn to running the company itself. At this stage, as you are rapidly rising, go back to the questions from the very first layer of the pyramid: What is your brand? What is your endgame? Everything you have been doing throughout this process has been about your brand. If you have a mentor, speak with him or her about how to take that next step. Remember to never get complacent. You need to ask yourself the same questions as the business owner or your manager: am I missing anything? Are my skills still sharp? Am I relevant? You still need that fire in your belly.

## If you are an aspiring entrepreneur:

Just as Des Jardins says, your end goal has always been to go out on your own. The timetable you set to achieve this goal could have taken longer or shorter than you anticipated, but at this level of the pyramid, you should be at the point where the reasons to do it surpass the reasons not to. As you embark on your new journey, reflect on Lisa's question: "How do I build a business by providing a service no one else has provided?" Whatever you answer, stick with it.

---

## FINAL THOUGHTS

Reaching your goal of world domination is exciting, but even after the leaders in this book all got there, they didn't stop reaching. Even today, they continue to dream new dreams. After all, the world we live in is constantly evolving. All good companies continue to innovate and push the envelope, even when they are at the top of their game. BlogHer may have achieved world domination, but its founders are not lying around gloating about their success. They continue to build their empire by using the lessons they have learned within each previous level of the pyramid.

Just as a real pyramid is connected from its apex all the way down to the foundation, all layers of the opportunity pyramid are pieces of a puzzle that join to help you achieve success. One missing piece and the pyramid is incomplete, weakened. That's how you need to look at the apex. It's more than just a peak. It's an invisible beam that extends through the entire structure all the way down to the foundation and anchors it. The lessons of the pyramid are many, and the results extraordinary. The decision is up to you: Are you ready to start building?

# 9

# Create Your Own Opportunity Pyramid

THROUGHOUT THIS BOOK, you have seen how some of the world's most successful business leaders have defined and seized opportunity by using the seven principles that make up the opportunity pyramid. It doesn't matter if you're a dreamer, a corporate executive, or a small-business owner—the opportunity pyramid *can* be applied to anyone. It is a model you can customize based on how you want to achieve your goals. My aim in writing this book is to show you that even personalities as different as Alan Mulally and Steve Case can do this, and to encourage you to discover how your own special traits can lead you to succeed.

No matter how you start out in life—the child of sharecroppers, a housewife, an executive with an Ivy League education—everyone creates his or her own path. The road to prosperity can be filled with potholes and detours, but you have the ability to fill the holes and create new roads. Success or failure begins with *you*. As David Rubenstein pointed out, "Hard work and perseverance—which may mean long hours—will generally enable me to achieve my desired goals, and may help to overcome other personal deficiencies or weaknesses."

No one ever said it was going to be easy, and no one in this world is entitled to success. You have to work hard and earn it. You just don't achieve success and say "I'm done." Case stressed to me: "It is a long and difficult road—there are ups and downs, moments of glory and moments of despair." He says, "To be a successful entrepreneur leading a team through such uncertainty, inner passion is a necessity. You have to believe in the objective—and care enough, with every fiber in your body—that you will weather the hard times in order to get to a new day." Do you "show up" every day? Give it your all? If you were on the receiving end of your work, would you be happy?

## ONE UNIVERSAL PYRAMID

What I find so interesting is that if you peel away all the stardom and success from these individuals and just look at the qualities they possess, you wouldn't be able to tell them apart. All of the individuals I have focused on in *Opportunity Knocking* have the same traits. That is what is so exciting. Knowledge of oneself and one's industry, conviction, determination, and willingness to risk are common to all of them. These traits are all free, and you can tap into them time and time again at no cost. The end result of all this hard work is personal satisfaction you can't put a price tag on. Happiness is the result of achieving success in the way you define it personally. Monetary reward is nice, but success can mean different things for different people, and that's OK.

When I look at my career, I see the pyramid traits I have employed since I started in the news business in the early nineties. For my foundation, I defined what kind of journalism I wanted to cover and I learned everything I could from the news veterans I worked with. I did everything from shooting and editing to reporting and anchoring. I wanted to learn how all the pieces of the news puzzle fit together. I then branched off to the assignment desk, creating stories, dispatching and assisting crews, and producing investigative pieces. Through the years, I have been presented with opportunities and asked myself this key question: What is best for me over the long term? Before I was hired at CNBC, I left local news to become the creator of a startup business show. At first I was nervous to leave a career I had known for over a decade, but my husband said to me, "You like to create special programming—you should try. You can always go back to local news if you want to." I thought about the long-term opportunities it could create for me (creating a program out of nothing, giving me more responsibility, challenging me in a new news genre—business news). I decided to take the plunge, and within six months of starting the job, I was approached by a

TV agent and asked if I would be interested in a job at CNBC. If I didn't take that opportunity at the startup business show, I would never be where I am today.

My contacts have emphasized to me over the years that passion not only drives them to achieve their goals, but also comforts them when things are tough. Nicky Pappadakis, a contact I interviewed for my book *Dynasties of the Sea*, once said to me, "If you do your job with a happy heart, it shows. The same goes for the opposite." I know so many people who are miserable with their jobs, and not only are they cancers to their organizations, but their performance is, at best, mediocre. If you love what you do, you excel. Ron Kruszewski advised, "Make career decisions based on enjoyment of the substance of the work rather than the level of compensation. People in careers they find meaningful find that the financial rewards usually follow." This is what happened with the founders of BlogHer. They all left successful careers because they were not happy. They wanted to be fulfilled. And guess what? Now they are both financially secure and happy.

I can honestly say I love my job. I love to challenge myself when trying to find the right person for a story and talking to contacts about different angles. How about you? Over the years, as I have developed and strengthened each layer of my pyramid, my confidence has helped me achieve my goals. My first goal was to work at a network news organization by 30. I achieved my goal at 29. At that time in my career, it was my "world domination" moment. My goals have since gotten bigger, but I know that with hard work I will be able to attain them.

That is *my* opportunity pyramid. How I have chosen to grow my brand and value and how I contribute to my organization *are* my business. Again, it all starts with knowing myself. What do I want to achieve? Those are the two biggest questions you have to ask; the course you take has to be tailored by you. You cannot expect someone to lay out your destiny for you. Did Ron Kruszewski and the founders of BlogHer take the same approach in building their companies? Absolutely not, but they share the traits of confidence, conviction, determination—and a thirst for more.

One of the biggest sources of enjoyment I have received over the years is meeting the entrepreneurs and dreamers of the world. It doesn't matter what size their bank accounts are, they all possess the same spark in their eyes, passion to succeed, and the willingness to dream. I think too often people sell themselves short. Doubting your abilities can be corrosive in building your opportunity pyramid. It can undermine your goals. The world can be a very unforgiving place, so why should you beat *yourself* up?

Believe in yourself. I personally love Lisa Stone's words of wisdom in this area: "Confidence is the heartbeat of beauty. The trick? To get there we have to fail and change. The courage to fail is irresistible to me." Courage is the byproduct of believing.

## NO GAP, NO DIFFERENCE

I want you to realize you *can* relate to an auto titan like Alan Mulally, an oil millionaire like Harold Hamm, and Internet entrepreneurs like the founders of BlogHer. If you are shaking your head in disbelief, then you've missed the point of this book. There is *no* gap between your goals and dreams and their goals and dreams. In fact, you all have the same goal: to be successful. The seven underlying pyramid principles are all the same, but tailored to an individual's personality and strengths. Elisa Camahort Page's mantra says it best: "Do the best that you can, until you can do better. None of us is perfect. But we should never do nothing because we can't do everything."

## LAY YOUR FOUNDATION

The key ingredient to building your foundation is honesty, which is essential for **knowing yourself**. All of the people featured in this book had to come to terms with their strengths and weaknesses in order to achieve their goals. Honesty can be tough, but it is necessary. Ron Kruszewski, one of the most direct CEOs I know, hit the nail on the head when he said, "People cannot fully recognize which are their best skills without first being comfortable recognizing their own weaknesses. Remarkably, this is often a significant barrier for persons of high intellect."

I have met highly intelligent, Ivy League–educated individuals who not only lack common sense, but also lack the honesty they need to look at themselves. If you think you are perfect, you are setting yourself up for a rude awakening. No one is without flaws, and you should always be learning and evolving from your own. The more confidence you develop, you will carry yourself better and be better able to handle whatever comes your way. I never stop learning from my successes or failures. There is something to take from every experience. I personally get inspiration from all different sources, including songs, like Martina McBride's "This One's for the Girls," in which she sings, "Every laugh line on your face made you who you are today." Your experiences define who you are based on how you handle them.

Making a list of your strengths and weaknesses can be helpful when you are building your foundation. It may sound silly, but it's a good exercise. Seeing things in black and white can sometimes make goals clearer. How do you want people to know you? Look at yourself as a brand. Here are just some examples of what questions you should ask yourself: If you work for an organization, how do you want your boss and colleagues to think of you? What expertise makes you invaluable to your organization? How can you strengthen your position? Kruszewski gave some unique insight into what he looks for in an employee, breaking down the important difference between mediocre performance and mediocre talent: "Marginally talented but dedicated people can be valuable employees. But mediocre performers are an organization's most expensive talent. Their presence keeps you from bringing in a good performer and their work product usually needs shoring up by others in a distracting manner."

If you are dreaming of a new career, make a timeline of goals so you can check off each accomplishment until you are ready to go out on your own. Work side jobs to help lay the foundation. As Des Jardins said: "Eventually, you make the leap. It's always the end goal. Not, 'I'm going to do this to see if it works and *then* I'm going to do it.' You always have that as your end goal." Remember that it took Des Jardins three tries before she successfully went out on her own. She didn't get discouraged, and neither should you.

## WHAT MAKES YOU SPECIAL?

Part of self-definition is knowing what sets you apart. In today's business environment, where competition can be fierce, you need to differentiate yourself by specializing. Knowing how to do three or four jobs well is good, but knowing how to do one job brilliantly is exceptional. It doesn't mean you shouldn't try different things and learn as much as you can, as I did when I started out—but keep an end goal in mind so you don't get sidetracked. Mulally summed the strategy up perfectly: "The essence of me is to contribute to a compelling vision. It's about meaningful accomplishments. I have always asked myself, 'What will I commit my life to?' It's that question that has been my steadfast foundation in how I have sought out and seized on opportunity."

These leaders all know what makes them special. You need to ask yourself what your competitive edge is. As Des Jardins stressed in our conversation, the founders of BlogHer continuously ask themselves, "What are we missing?" Once you define *who* you are and what *your* specialty is, you need to create a checklist to run possible opportunities against. All of the people in this book have their own specialized lists to define opportunity, and so should you. You want to make sure you are taking on an opportunity that will help you thrive.

All of the leaders I spoke with told me that, while their approaches to opportunities remain constant, they also recognize that the environments in which they operate are constantly changing. They all stressed the need to be nimble. That's why Des Jardins says you can't get too wedded to what something will look like: "You just have to go with it. You have to remain true to it. Give up on what it looks like, and let it grow."

Schlosstein echoed that sentiment when he said, "It is critical to pull on your own strengths, and then adapt to the world as it changes." Kruszewski added to this thought by stressing that an opportunity can pass you by if you lack vision. He evaluates the opportunities when they present themselves, running them against his goals, and if the opportunities fit where he wants to take his company, he takes them.

It doesn't matter if you're leading a startup like BlogHer or a large corporation like those run by Schlosstein, Hamm, Mulally, Kruszewski, or Rubenstein. Success depends on the culture of a business; it's the rebar that holds the layers of the opportunity pyramid together. Culture is not only your shared beliefs, but your way of life. Alan Mulally's One Ford culture and Rubenstein's One Carlyle culture are two examples. How do you define your culture? What do you do to nourish it?

If you are working at a company, how would you characterize the company's culture? Do you feel invested in where you're working? All of the leaders in this book agree they could not afford to have employees who are not wholly committed to the company's culture. Both Mulally and Kruszewski even said they lost talent because those employees didn't fit into their organizations' cultures. Leaders like Mulally and Kruszewski do not view the loss of such employees as negative, because those employees didn't enhance the organization in the first place. It doesn't matter if you are the employer or the employee—having a successful culture begins and ends with value. Every person in an organization should bring value and passion to the table. Creating a positive culture is key to all these leaders' foundations—as Schlosstein described it, "You need to be a long term believer in the things that enhance productivity." Even the tchotchkes and posters in Carlyle's offices have helped foster their One Carlyle message. Productivity is nurtured in a variety of ways. It's like a welcome sign or plaques with sayings that you put up in your home. How are you trying to set the tone?

## THE PASSION TO LEARN

With a strong identity and culture fortifying the base of your company or career, the next level is **building your knowledge**. By doing so, you are able to operate in a more nimble way, because you open yourself to new possibilities instead of being stuck in one mode. Building your knowledge goes back to examining the package of skills you present, and then deciding how to expand them.

So how would you personalize this level of the pyramid? Some options are keeping up on trends by reading, taking a new college course or two, networking, and finding a mentor. When Harold Hamm looked at his strengths and weaknesses, he realized he needed to learn more in order to build his energy empire. He was a sponge, learning as much as he could from others. Once he had the financial means, he carefully chose courses that could help him expand his business. He shows you that you do not need an MBA from Harvard to be successful. Microsoft founder Bill Gates was a college dropout. Ideas and execution are everything.

What excites you? Do you want to write a children's book? Do you dream of opening a wine bar or daycare? Are you holding back from taking your career to the next level? Go to the library and do research. Maybe you're a visionary and have a product you want to start selling. If so, learn more about how to market it and the demographic you are hoping to target. Make time to do it. As a mother of three busy children, I carve out my "me time" at five a.m. or after the kids go to bed. You have to want it, taste it, be driven. That fire in your belly has to be so hot it consumes you. As Des Jardins said, "Consider doing it now. Note I didn't say do it, but *consider* doing it. Asking yourself to consider takes the pressure off acting right away, but the seeds are subconsciously planted." Have you given yourself the option to do that? Don't you owe that to yourself?

Another way to build your knowledge is to become a consummate "brain picker," like Kruszewski. Don't be afraid to find a mentor. You are never too old. If you are truly interested in their field, most people are very happy to help you. I have gone out of my way with interns or former colleagues if I see that sparkle in their eye, that passion to learn.

## LASER-LIKE FOCUS

None of the leaders in this book were hampered by doubters. They **defined their opportunity strategies and stuck with them**. What I like so much about Ron Kruszewski is that his plan is not typical, but when you really think about it, his three-step approach to analyzing opportunities *is* a plan. The way you go about leading is a plan. How would you describe your leadership style? Is it forward-thinking? Encouraging?

While Kruszewski doesn't like to be confined by the conventional, he keeps himself open to all opportunities based on his "no five-year plan" approach. But that doesn't mean he's reckless. He has a structure in place to assess risk. His unconventional leadership style works because he knows what his organization stands for and what strengths it brings to the table. His foundation is strong and his knowledge in the areas in which he operates is solid, so he's able to look at the world as a blank canvas.

## LOVE WHAT YOU DO

What fuels the growth of the opportunity is **passion**, as I've mentioned before. All of these leaders truly love what they do. Mulally's passion is infectious. I have friends who work for him, and they said he creates an amazing driving force that you can't help but get swept up in. When you speak with him, you get energized. CEOs like AutoNation's Mike Jackson enjoy working with him because of Mulally's dedication, critical thinking, and devotion. These types of leaders inspire. This inspiration then motivates workers. Passion sets the tone, the agenda, the execution. How you do you set a passionate example?

When Harold Hamm was first introduced to the oil industry, he knew right then and there he wanted to be a part of it. It didn't matter that he had no money, no formal education in the field. Instead of viewing those headwinds as obstacles, Hamm forged his own path.

He learned as he moved up the ranks and from those around him. He showed that if you love what you do, you excel.

Passion and happiness go hand in hand. One of the reasons why Des Jardins, Stone, and Camahort Page of BlogHer were unhappy in their previous careers—even though they were all successful—is because they lacked the passion they were craving and they wanted to be fulfilled. In blogging, they found that passion. It enabled them to create a product that they themselves wanted to use. They connected with their audience because they *were* their audience.

Passion is one of the three Ps in Steve Case's business strategy and is the fuel behind the dossier of companies he has created, helped nurture, and given seed money to. Passion also attracts others who are passionate. Remember what Case said: "You need to have a team of people around you that you enjoy being with, trust, and can rely on. When the going gets tough, you want to be surrounded by individuals who share a common purpose and outlook—people who keep you grounded when things are going well and rally together when times are tough."

## CONCENTRATE

There are defining moments in everyone's life. They can either be positive or negative. It's the strategies you employ in response to these moments that determine your fate. As Jack Welch once said, "Face reality as it is, not as it was or as you wish it to be."

Success doesn't happen overnight. It takes time, and everyone in this book obtained it by **staying the course**. Remember what Rubenstein said about the kinds of concentration challenges we face today versus those of our forefathers. The distraction of texts, emails, and calls can be overwhelming, especially in a business that runs 24/7. For example, if there is breaking news on a weekend, I need to jump in as well as tend to my three kids and other family activities. I have to do it all without impacting the quality of my work. I'm a multitasker and I thrive on challenge, but it can be hard to keep focus on the task at hand. I stay the course by going through my checklists to assess the situation, then addressing how I will react and execute. The difference between "juggling" everything and true multitasking is the ability to prioritize and keep the focus on each task in order to do it right.

## FACE THE CHALLENGE

Focus goes hand in hand with the next level of the opportunity pyramid: **execution.** This part of the pyramid relies heavily on planning, so make sure you have all the details checked and double-checked before you begin. Many of my CEO contacts tell me you need to have plans A, B, and C ready to go, because it might become necessary to change course. In Hamm's words: "Planning—planning—execution. Planning is integral to good execution. People who come in with their hair on fire irk me. Poor planning on their part does not necessarily constitute an emergency on my part." During the financial crisis and when I started writing *Thriving in the New Economy*, Mike Jackson, chairman and CEO of AutoNation, stressed to me the need to have flawless execution and a worst-case scenario plan. He had a financial crisis plan ready for his company years before it was actually needed, and he wasn't afraid to execute when, unfortunately, the economic and business world did start collapsing around him.

Emotions can play a big part in the success or failure of execution. They must be kept in check. All of the leaders I have met both in and out of the business world, have a matter-of-fact level-headedness about them. Keeping your cool is a must. If you get frazzled it doesn't help the situation. It's hard not to let your emotions get the best of you but it doesn't matter if you work for an organization or you are the owner of a business—showing stress in the way you are leading a challenge does not exude confidence. If you do not execute properly, all your hard work has been for nothing.

When it comes to planning a strategy and then executing, there are four steps to take away from the stories you've just read:

- **Acknowledge the situation:** All of the leaders profiled in this book have taken a candid look at the business landscape they are in and asked themselves where they could make a meaningful mark.

- **Assess the strengths you have to tackle the situation:** In order to make that mark, these leaders look at how they can set themselves apart. From private equity to Internet entrepreneurship, all of these leaders created a niche and grew it based on what they were good at.

- **Make a list of the likely scenarios and how you plan to execute:** For example, like Harold Hamm, look at the challenges facing your industry and then ask yourself how to create opportunities to circumvent disaster. For Hamm, this meant creating new ways to drill oil out of the ground.

· **Take the challenge head on:** None of the businesspeople profiled shied away when the challenges swelled around them. For example, Alan Mulally always returned to his company's mission statement when a difficult decision was to be made. The culture he created at Ford helped the once-beleaguered automaker rise out of the ashes like a phoenix. Remember that the culture you have built up as part of your pyramid will sustain you through challenges. Lee Iacocca sums this up perfectly, "In the end, all business operations can be reduced to three words: people, product, and profits. Unless you've got a good team, you can't do much with the other two."[17]

## ENVISION YOUR CAPSTONE

Getting to the apex of the opportunity pyramid does not happen overnight. But when your goal is **world domination**, why would you expect it to be fast—or easy? Building the great pyramids in Egypt was no simple task. That is why I chose this structure to be an icon of the path to prosperity. According to archaeologists, when the pyramids were constructed, the capstone (also called the top-stone), was not only the last to be placed, but was the most important part of the structure because the apex was said to be an invisible pole connecting each layer to the base. This distinction was made symbolically by fabricating this top piece from gold or a special stone. The apex of the opportunity pyramid is embellished with the fruits of success.

Since you have your own pyramid, what would your capstone be? If you personalize and visualize it, the capstone can help you focus on your path. Look at what Rubenstein has done. The tchotchkes on the desks in all of the Carlyle offices around the world and the posters that flank their lunchroom walls help keep employees focused on achieving their goals. But you can even write down your apex on a Post-it note. It doesn't have to be grand. Just stick it on your wall, at your desk, or in your wallet—anywhere you'll see it and be reminded of why you are working so hard.

As you are growing your business or career, you may come to a crossroads. Taking that next big step could lead you out of your comfort zone. Are you willing? Or do you want to stay where you are? The found-ers of BlogHer didn't want to waste their sacrifices and hard work by passing the baton to someone who didn't share their passion, and thus let a competitor surpass them. Remember what Des Jardins said to me, "If someone was going to achieve world domination in this space, it was going to be us and *not* someone else." If you created something, would you be satisfied with handing that baton to someone else? If you are that's fine, but for many it's not. After all my years meeting with amaz-ing entrepreneurs, I have likened business owners, no matter what the size of their organization, to athletes. They are competitive. They want to be on top. Second-best is not good enough.

## SMALL IS THE NEW BIG

The genesis of many businesses is small. The founders of BlogHer took out home-equity loans. Harold Hamm started his business with a single truck. But these leaders' courage, perseverance, and determination were as important as the money they invested.

That said, remember that having a vested interest in your business makes a huge difference. Every dollar counts when you are spending your own money. It can be an agonizing process, but it's all part of your journey. Many of my contacts who are entrepreneurs tell me that when they use their own money, they are more conservative in invest-ing. They think more about the long term, rather than thinking quarter to quarter. As Rubenstein reminds us, "A focus on long-term goals will produce far greater benefits than a focus on short-term goals."

## REBUILDING WHAT'S BROKEN

Sometimes when companies reach their apex, they lose their way. The layers of the opportunity pyramid weaken and crumble, forcing its col-lapse. In cases like these, leaders have to rebuild, as Alan Mulally did with Ford's opportunity pyramid. A pyramid with all levels based on the principles of the company's founder Henry Ford in combination with Mulally's strategy and execution has successfully brought Ford back to an even grander status. In order to fix what was broken, Mulally had to take a hard look at the company and relate each and every decision back to what he wanted Ford to be. What do *you* want to be? What do you want your company to do? In order to fix something, a bar has to be set and not refigured constantly. You need to set the standard and achieve to meet that standard.

## HUMILITY

Finally, when success is attained, what separates the winners and losers is their level of humility. Nothing is worse than meeting someone successful who is not a nice person. I have been disappointed more times than I care to admit.

The people in this book, however, are different. When you look at the quotations I have collected, each of these leaders discusses humility. From Harold Hamm, who says "I try to practice humility on a daily basis," to David Rubenstein, who reminds us, "If good fortune should strike, it is important to give back much of that good fortune to help others ... reach their own objectives and to achieve some measure of good fortune as well," these leaders have never forgotten where they came from. Their pyramids are stronger because of that.

Now is the time for *you* to look within. So roll up your sleeves and get ready for the dig of your lifetime. Your future is waiting.

# Afterword

M Y LIBRARIES ARE filled with business books that are either "gee-whiz" stories about some resounding business success or "how-to" manuals recounting a business leader's description of what he or she regards as a universal formula for a successful career. *Opportunity Knocking* is instead a unique combination of both genres, plus the penetrating insights gleaned by Lori Ann LaRocco from her years of interacting with global leaders as a producer of CNBC's *Squawk Box.*

The book begins with a unique and original conceptualization developed by the author. This is a seven-layer opportunity pyramid one must climb up to achieve *über* success. At ground level is your foundation, or knowing yourself. The pyramid then builds through generic layers—knowledge, strategy, passion, staying the course, and execution—until it reaches the top, which is modestly captioned "world domination." At first glance, these may seem like ordinary buzzwords, but Lori Ann has gone through her unparalleled Rolodex and selected world-renowned business leaders to contribute personal vignettes, each illustrating a different layer of the pyramid. Because of her experience with these leaders, the author was able to figure out which person's career achievement would best illustrate each layer of the pyramid. Even more impressive is that iconic figures as diverse as Ford Motor chief executive Alan Mulally; Carlyle founding partner David Rubenstein; Harold Hamm, the wildcatter who pioneered the Bakken oil field in North Dakota; and others were willing to share autobiographical anecdotes to illustrate the point. To tie everything together, Lori Ann has appended at the end of each success story a "Building Your Pyramid" section that helps readers to apply to their own lives the lessons they have just learned.

Not too surprisingly, this high alpha group does have some shared basic personality traits. Each has a strong intellect and takes calculated risks, is passionate about the enterprise, and is persistent, almost to the point of obsession. It was fascinating to learn how tailored iterations of individual mental states were applied to the defining moments of that person's career, and to learn of the corporate cultures that were created as a result. Even more intriguing is how each interacted with one or more layers of Lori Ann's pyramid.

The engaging style of the book makes it a quick, easy read, and its content makes it a must-read for a wide audience: students, business school professors, those in the business community who aspire to be on the Forbes 400 list, those already on the list who want to propel themselves even higher on it, and most of all, competing executives who were defeated by the people in this book.

Had the pharaohs known Lori Ann, they would have stopped the Great Pyramid at 7 layers, not the 210 they actually built. On a more personal note, if I had read the book when I was younger, I could have avoided some earlier missteps in my own career. This book is a truly singular achievement in the annals of business journalism.

**Wilbur L. Ross**

*Wilbur L. Ross is the chairman and CEO of WL Ross & Co., LLC.*

# Acknowledgments

THIS BOOK HAS been an incredible journey and I have been very fortunate to have a wonderful foundation of people who have supported me. Thank you to my wonderful family—your understanding and support mean so much to me. I appreciate all your love and patience. You are my world.

To my friends Anna "Ania" Sharygina, Matthew J. Barbis, and Kirsten Chang, thank you for reading the book and giving me your honest critiques. I'm always a big believer in having a second or third set of eyes reviewing my work, and your honest feedback was very helpful. You are wonderful and your friendship and time spent on my book is deeply appreciated.

To Cynthia Zigmund, my literary agent: you are the best! Your passion, dedication, and editorial insight are priceless. Thank you for being there every step of the way. You are just amazing. Thank you Doug Seibold and Agate Publishing for taking on this project. I truly appreciate the opportunity.

Finally, I would like to thank CNBC president and CEO Mark Hoffman and senior vice president and editor in chief of business news Nik Deogun for supporting me in writing this book. To my boss, *Squawk Box* executive producer Matt Quayle, thank you for supporting me and giving me the green light for my book projects. I truly appreciate your support. I'd also like to thank Brian Steel, SVP of public relations at CNBC. Thank you for allowing me to continue to build my own opportunity pyramid.

# Notes

1. BlackRock, "Who We Are," December 31, 2012, http://www.blackrock.com /corporate/en-us/about-us.

2. The Forbes 400, *Forbes*, September 2013.

3. Source: PIRA Energy Group.

4. Source: US Energy Information Administration.

5. Philip LeBeau, "Toyota Passes GM To Become #1," Behind the Wheel with Phil LeBeau, CNBC.com, January 21, 2009, http://www.cnbc.com /id/28772779.

6. Source: Ford Motor Company.

7. Tim Arango, "In Retrospect: How the AOL–Time Warner Merger Went So Wrong," *New York Times,* January 10, 2010, http://www.nytimes .com/2010/01/11/business/media/11merger.html?_r=1&adxnnl=1 &pagewanted=all&adxnnlx=1382371260-KS4Tucne5SuZEQxQQRrxaA.

8. "Levin Is Sorry for Creating AOL Time Warner," DealBook, *New York Times,* January 4, 2010, http://dealbook.nytimes.com/2010/01/04/levin -apologizes-for-aol-time-warner-a-decade-later/.

9. "Who's Sorry Now? Steve Case, For One," DealBook, *New York Times,* July 24, 2006, http://dealbook.nytimes.com/2006/07/24/whos-sorry-now-steve -case-for-one/.

10. Source: Stifel Financial Corp.

11. Ibid.

12. Ibid.

13. Ibid.

14. Source: The Carlyle Group.

15. Ibid.

16. Nielsen Site Census, May 2013.

17. Lee Iacocca, *Iacocca: An Autobiography* (New York: Bantam, 1984).

# Appendix

## Lessons from the Leaders

I AM THE TYPE of reader who loves to jot down quotes that speak to me. In this book, I shared some of them where I thought they would be appropriate. I also made a list of some of the quotes I found most powerful and inspirational, which I'm sharing here. Think of them as the bricks that are used to build the individual layers of the opportunity pyramid.

### RALPH SCHLOSSTEIN

"There is always a 'new normal' and every business has to adapt in order to continue to be successful."

"It is critical to pull on your own strengths and then adapt to the world as it changes."

"You need a clear strategy that is responsive to both the environment in which you are operating and the relative strengths of your business. If you do one without the other, you lose. If you create a business plan that is not relevant to the world as it is today, failure is probable."

"If you figure out what is going to work today, you need to make sure your decisions are competitive for that specific strategy. If you are not competitive you could also lose."

"You can't ignore the financial objectives."

"You have to clearly look at what skill set or talent pool is needed to succeed in a meaningful way in that opportunity."

"The fundamental building block to good execution is a realistic view of what your company is good at."

## HAROLD HAMM

"My entire business plan simply was, if I did a better job at a fair price I would end up with most of the work."

"Persistence is everything in this business.... It certainly helped me develop the tenacity and all of the habits of being a great entrepreneur. Without these qualities, you couldn't make it in this business."

"I developed laser-like focus. I locked on to my dream and didn't quit until I got there."

"I never gave up. Sometimes things don't go your way, but they can be the life shapers to be able to take on the next challenge. It is necessary for survival. Hardship sometimes is just as necessary as accomplishments. If it is too easy, you don't learn the skills you need in order not to give up and achieve success."

## ALAN MULALLY

"The essence of me is to contribute to a compelling vision. It's about meaningful accomplishments. I have always asked myself, 'What will I commit my life to?' It's that question that has been my steadfast foundation in how I have sought out and seized on opportunity."

"You don't wait for an opportunity. It doesn't come to you when you are just sitting in a room."

"You never want an improvement to pass you by, because you need that improvement every month, every year, in order to continue on your path to continuously improve and deliver that compelling vision."

"You know you can't fool anybody. Without leadership sharing the same vision and communicating about how they would execute, the One Ford plan would cease to exist."

## STEVE CASE

"In all of my business endeavors I have made it a point to hire the most talented and passionate people. Surrounding yourself and your company with talent is essential to grow. You can't do it alone."

"There's an African proverb that says if you want to go quickly, go alone, but if you want to go far, you must go together. I like big ideas that take some time to develop, and can only be developed by a team. Entrepreneurs must be talent scouts all the time, always on the lookout for people to add to their team."

"To be a successful entrepreneur leading a team through such uncertainty, inner passion is a necessity. You have to believe in the objective—and care enough, with every fiber in your body—that you will weather the hard times in order to get to a new day."

"If you have a talented group of people that are passionate and well led, I don't think there's a limit on what can be achieved in terms of building a great organization or a great brand."

"I see it as the responsibility of every successful entrepreneur to act as a mentor and coach for the next generation of entrepreneurs."

## RON KRUSZEWSKI

"I have never told my employees that I know everything. I don't, and I'm open to change."

"Opportunity presents itself *to* you. You are never sure where it is going to come from. The hallmark of opportunity is that you are out there with a plan saying you are going to do a specific thing, and you look for just that opportunity and execute on that. That's not taking advantage of opportunity."

"I spend my life *evaluating* opportunity. I don't spend my life trying to *create* an opportunity. That is a very important distinction. It is a difference between believing a business plan is 'to do' something, versus letting opportunity come *to* you."

"To run a business this way you have to invest a lot of authority with your key people. You motivate them, and they like it. This positive reinforcement builds the culture."

"Good leaders are always thinking, evaluating."

"Once your opportunities come to you and you corral them and you are stable, I believe you need to be very strict on the business models, expense controls, and running the business in order to successfully grow your business."

## DAVID RUBENSTEIN

"You need to make sure you have a game plan that has been vetted, as well as an execution plan so you can deploy your capital effectively."

"Time is an important factor when improving a company."

"I don't think it is always good to have a short-term investment horizon. If you are able to get a long-term horizon, you will probably do well because you are going to counter the general population."

"Great fortunes have been made, and will always be made, depending on what a government does. If you take a look at the greatest investments ever made, many of these investments have taken advantage of either a legislative change or regulatory change. If someone can figure out what those changes will be in advance, they'll probably do reasonably well if they pursue the right niches."

"If you are afraid of making a mistake and losing money, then you can't be in the deals world."

## LISA STONE, ELISA CAMAHORT PAGE, AND JORY DES JARDINS

**Camahort Page:** "When you work for other people there's a point when your authority ends, and you have to act based on the decisions you may not agree with because they are coming from people who are over your head."

**Des Jardins:** "It was so powerful doing my own thing that it got to the point that the risk of not doing it outweighed the risk of doing it."

**Des Jardins:** "Eventually you make the leap. It's always the end goal. Not, 'I'm going to take this small step, see if it works, and *then* I'm going to be an entrepreneur.' You always have that leap as your *end* goal. It may take longer than you think, and you may stay in a corporation for a long time, or do something other than your new business, but it's always your end goal to leave and do your business full time."

**Stone:** "Ask yourself, 'How do I build a business by providing a service that no one else has provided?'"

**Des Jardins:** "We always ask ourselves, 'What are we missing?' And we will continue to ask that question. It is a question anyone who has had success in an area should be asking themselves—'Will I remain relevant?' We have never rested on our laurels. It is a constant tapping process."

**Des Jardins:** "You can't get too wedded to what something will look like. You just have to go with change while remaining true to your mission. Give up on what it looks like, and let it grow."

**Des Jardins:** "If someone was going to achieve world domination in this space, it was going to be us and *not* someone else."

# Index

# About the Author

ORI ANN LaROCCO is an American journalist and the author of *Dynasties of the Sea* (Marine Money International, 2012) and *Thriving in the New Economy* (Wiley, 2010). As senior talent producer at CNBC, Lori Ann has the ear of some of the world's biggest business minds. She has been working at the network since 2000, when she was first hired as one of Maria Bartiromo's producers on her first prime-time show, *Market Week*. Lori Ann has produced and booked interviews with some of the biggest names in business, garnering her trust and respect from Wall Street to Washington. Lori Ann's relationships with top business leaders have earned her first access to business deals in the billions of dollars, enabling her show, *Squawk Box*, to break the news first. Prior to joining CNBC, Lori Ann was an anchor, reporter, and assignment editor in various local news stations across the country.